ANGLER'S MOON

Leo Walmsley

Angler's Moon

Memories of Fish, Fishing and Fishermen

BY

Leo Walmsley

The Walmsley Society

First published in 1965 by Hamish Hamilton Ltd.

This edition published in 2008 by
The Walmsley Society
www.walmsleysoc.org

ISBN 0-9534449-4-5

British Library Cataloguing-in-Publication Data:
A catalogue record is available for this book
from the British Library.

Printed and bound by

www.BookPrintingUK.com
Peterborough

FOR SELINA

1

IT is a well-known saying that the biggest fish always gets away! There are few fishermen, be they professional, or expert sporting anglers, or summer holiday-makers casting their baited lines from pier ends or hire boats into sea or lake or river, who have not had that bitter experience: the trophy fish, to be exultantly displayed to envious fellow fishers, to be proudly weighed, photographed, perhaps to be stuffed, or plaster-cast and put in a glass case, the fish to dream about—the fish that got away!

Although Yorkshire born and bred I have lived for many years at Fowey, in Cornwall. From an angler's point of view Fowey has the great advantage of a landlocked deep-water harbour and an extensive river estuary from which branch several tidal creeks. Except in violent storms, one can fish in any sort of weather the whole year round, either from boat or jetty or from the rocks at the harbour mouth or along the coast.

For those who have the time, the patience, and the optimism, even though nine out of ten of their baits are removed from hooks by shore crabs, there are flounders and plaice, dabs and sole to be caught bottom-fishing from an anchored boat in the harbour. In late spring the bass come in from deep water, to feed on the sand eels which swarm in the middle reaches of the estuary. These, next to salmon and salmon trout (which may be caught by rod and line in the fresh water of the River Fowey under licence), are the sporting angler's fish supreme. Using light tackle, a live sand eel or prawn or even 'artificial' for bait, they are taken by slow trolling or by streaming from anchored boats on the flood or the ebb tide. They are gallant fighters, and are delicious to eat. Two-pounders are an average, but they can run up to fourteen or more.

Yet there is more in fishing than the catching of fish. In spite of the estuary bass—my biggest is eight pounds—I have a preference for the open sea, outside the harbour mouth east or west along the cliff-bound coast, cliffs which in shape and colour are among the loveliest in Great Britain. They fall—except where they are broken by shingly coves—sheer into a relatively deep water to a rocky bottom giving anchorage to a forest of kelp and oar weed whose gently swaying fronds are visible in calm weather when the water has the transparency of polished plate-glass.

Such conditions by day with the sun shining are not favourable for the angler. The big fish have a habit of privacy. Otherwise they would not have grown to be big, with so many enemies eager to devour them from the moment they are hatched. If they are close in, gorged with their night's feast on sand eels or sprats, they wisely keep to the shelter of the umbrageous weeds, probably asleep, but with a weather eye open and reflexively alert, not to be fooled into thinking that a live rag worm unnaturally impaled on a piece of bent steel tied to a thin yet visible length of synthetic catgut, or a feather also tied to hook or line, or a piece of rubber tube designed to look like a sand eel are anything but what they are.

If such a fish could by magic be transformed in human shape so that it could examine the showcases of a modern fishing-tackle shop it would be impressed and flattered by the variety of the devices designed to lure it to destruction: the stacks of shining rods, with agate rings and chromium-plated mountings; the folding landing nets and gaffs: the creels, the live-bait boxes, the paternosters and sinkers, the patent casting reels which look as though they might play pop music when you wind the handle.

There are lines galore and all sizes and shapes of hooks. There are pickled sand eels and pickled prawns and rag worms; prawns and shore crabs, made in exact facsimile of the real thing, of pliable rubber-like plastic; glittering spinners; silvered spoon baits, and a device which functions like the paravane used by the Navy to sweep mines and which automatically rises to the surface when a fish is hooked: all designed to lure anglers as much as the fish themselves. And it is possible that the angler, having paid five bob for one of those so attractive-looking plastic prawns, will snag it among the weed or rock first time overboard. The laugh is so often on the fish!

It is pleasant to row or drift along in a boat on a summer sea close in to those fantastically sculptured and tinted cliffs of Fowey, to the incessant sound of the gulls which haunt them: to look down over the side of the boat, watching the swarms of jelly-fish sailing by like gala balloons, or Chinese lanterns, and to speculate, as an angler, as to what is going on below the masking weed, to picture say a monster pollack or bass, static except for a gentle vibration of its pectoral fins, or an occasional propulsive wag of its tail to mark time against the current; confidently secure, and not to be fooled by man until darkness falls, or when heavy rains cause a spate of the Fowey

River so that the close-in sea becomes muddied and opaque.

Angling may be an obsession with a man. Indeed there have been periods in my life when, domestically unattached for reasons which need not be dwelt upon, it has dominated my mind and activities so as to approach the condition of a vice, like drug taking and alcoholism. But I am happily married, with a high-spirited, eight-year-old daughter Selina, and both she and my wife, with reservations, share my addiction to boats and my favourite pastime, which has the pull over all other British sports in that it produces excellent food.

True that there are huntin' and shootin' . But only a wealthy landowner with the paid co-operation of gamekeepers and beaters, specially trained dogs, expensive weapons and ammunition, can be said to produce food: grouse, pheasants, partridges, woodcock, snipe and hares, and these only for the tables of the rich. Only the farmer whose hedgerows and warrens have not been decimated by myxomatosis can indulge his favourite winter sport of rabbit shooting. The foxhunter does not eat the fox he hunts, although opponents of the sport may think that this should be obligatory: that instead of the custom of 'blooding', the carcase of the slain animal should be rescued from the hounds and ceremoniously cut into pieces by the Master of Hounds, to be handed around to those huntsmen who are in at the kill—ladies first—to be chewed, or gnawed and swallowed, only bits of fur to be spat out.

I have said that my family share my addiction with reservations. I don't expect them to endure its occasional discomforts: 'sitting', as Rebecca West remarked in a notice she wrote about *Three Fevers,* 'sitting sodden in a boat hauling at wet lines while the horizon leaps and charges like a bull'. When they go fishing they want and expect to catch fish, and if they don't they get bored. They do not appreciate that half the delight of the dedicated angler in his sport is the anticipation. The long wait—and it may be hours—makes more exciting the climax of the hooked fish. Besides, on an idyllic summer day there are counter-attractions. The chances are that we would be on our way to one of our favourite coves, either in our motor boat *Amanda* or the dinghy, with food and drink ready for a picnic: to swim and bask in the sun, to climb over the rocks and search the crevices for crabs or lobsters, the pools for gaudy sea-slugs and anemones, starfish and urchins.

If we were in *Amanda* we would take a more seaward course to our destination and have a trolling line overboard for mackerel, perhaps the most beautiful in shape and markings and colour of all British fish but also the silliest for they will snap at any sort of bait so long as it is moving: spinner, feather, or a strip of skin cut from another mackerel, even a bare hook.

At certain seasons of the year they occur in vast shoals, feeding voraciously on the even vaster shoals of herring or pilchard fry. But when they lose contact with their favourite prey, they break up into smaller groups seeking other foods, so that there is always a chance of getting an odd one or two. Nothing would excite and delight Selina more than to feel the fierce tug on the line, to haul in with the fish darting from side to side, fighting all the way, then to lift it safely inboard; although she would avert her eyes when I unhooked it, and gave it the merciful *coup de grace.* A freshly caught mackerel, split open kipper-fashion and grilled over a driftwood fire would make a perfect contribution to our picnic.

But the weather conditions implied by Dame Rebecca's quoted remark are those which, within reason, are propitious for serious fishing: an overcast sky, a not-too-heavy swell, the water clouded by recent rain. Such were the conditions when I set out one evening with high hopes of encountering some of the big pollack I had enviously seen my friend Bill Haley, doyen of the local professionals, off-loading from his boat on Fowey's Town Quay. It was early spring, before the coming of the deep-water bass.

We live about half a mile from the harbour mouth, with *Amanda* on a permanent mooring, the dinghy secured to what is locally known as a frape, an endless cable running through pulleys, one fixed ashore, the other to a submerged anchor. For the fishing I had in mind I proposed to use the dinghy, for although a splendid sea boat, *Amanda* rolls uncomfortably in a swell unless taking it head-on and at least half-speed, too fast for pollack. To save time and energy, however, I boarded *Amanda,* and with the dinghy in tow, made for the harbour mouth.

On the opposite side of the harbour to Fowey is the smaller township of Polruan, whose narrow streets and alleys clustered on a steep hillside have much in common with my native Yorkshire village, although here the cottage roofs are pearly grey slate, and not brick red. The seafront of Polruan curves in as it approaches the harbour mouth, and terminates in a cliff surmounted by the ruins of an ancient castle. In the lee of this cliff is a safe anchorage clear of the shipping fairway and the tidal current. The water is deep, the bottom soft mud.

I dropped *Amanda's* anchor, hauled the dinghy

alongside, got in, and checked my gear. It was a special occasion, for I was going to try out a brand new rod my wife had presented to me to replace the old ash butt and greenheart top one I had treasured since my Yorkshire days and had broken beyond repair. This new rod was made of fibre-glass, allegedly unbreakable, supple as a whip. My reel was an ordinary one with a hundred yards of synthetic gut with a guaranteed breaking strain of twelve pounds. My trace, if it could be designated as such, was simply six feet of the same line but attached to it with a swivel, and above this a light sliding lead sinker, with a rubber stop so that the lead could be moved well up to the line when trolling but would slide back when reeling in. My bait was rag worm. I had a landing net, and as an extra precaution a gaff, and I saw that all this gear was now in the dinghy.

Trolling in a small boat you stand in the stern, with the rod in one hand, while you scull with a single oar; or you use both oars and fix your rod at an angle against the gunwhale or over the stern with the butt between your legs. This is the method I prefer when there is a swell. You keep your eyes on the rod tip, and when it jerks you smartly pull the oars inboard and take the rod in your hands.

I was very hopeful. Conditions were ideal. There was no wind. The swell was the aftermath of a moderate south-wester and in the lee of the cliff was scarcely noticeable. I decided that before casting off from *Amanda* I would bait the hook and pay the line overboard. It would stream out as soon as I was under way. But I forgot to adjust the sliding lead, which instead of being at least twelve feet up from the swivel and the trace, was only the length of the trace from the baited hook, which sank straight down to the bottom where the voracious shore crabs swarmed. The line went slack. I'd have to wind in again and see that the bait was untouched before starting to fish.

I reeled in the slack and felt the slight weight of the lead as it left the bottom. I got no farther. The line tightened, the rod bent. The hook was fast. I paid out the line a little, reeled in again and gave it a gentle jerk. The hook was still fast. I looked around and saw that there was no other moored boat near me. I could not have fouled the cable. There was no rock at the bottom, no oar weed. But it might be an old lost mooring or anchor I had fouled. It looked as though I would have to break the line, and put on a new trace hook, swivel and sinker.

I tried jerking again. Nothing gave. I tightened the line and increased the pressure, with the rod now bending almost into a semicircle, and suddenly the weight slackened, and with the rod nearly straight I reeled in about three feet of line, And then came a mighty tug, that almost wrenched the rod from my grasp, with a wriggle that could not possibly have been caused by an inanimate object. *It was a fish!*

With one finger on the reel as a brake, I let the line sink, for I had felt the power in that tug and realised that it would be impossible to haul in without some assistance from the fish itself. I must coax it upwards. I kept the line taut, waited a short spell. Then I started jerking, gently at first, then harder. The line slackened. I reeled in furiously until I felt its weight, and I must have gained at least a fathom when it gave another wriggling tug and I had to give way. It was down at the bottom again.

I took a prayerful breather, controlling the too-fast beating of my heart. I was aware that my hands were trembling as I re-started the jerks. Up it came again, a steady drag now but well within the breaking strain limit of the line. Clearly it was swimming, reluctantly and partly yielding to my pull. But I did not mistake this for a complete surrender.

The water here was about fifteen feet, too turgid however for me to see more than a few feet down, and as yet the fish could not be more than six feet from the bottom. I went on winding very slowly, the rod almost a semicircle. I dared to raise the tip of it, and was able to increase the speed of the wind for a few turns, but the drag was still heavy and I returned to the slow wind.

Slowly, slowly, inch by inch the fish was rising to the surface, still exerting a heavy drag, but rising vertically with no variation into a horizontal movement. I had no clue as to what species it was. I guessed that it could not be a bass, which like a mackerel always darts from side to side. That it was a fish, and a huge one, I had no doubt whatever, for the drag it was exerting could only be a fraction of its out-of-water weight.

Inch by inch! I could feel the thumping of my heart as I continued to wind. I gasped when suddenly the line slackened and the rod sprang back from bow shape to straight. *Had I lost it?* I reeled in the slack, recovering at least a fathom, and to my relief felt the drag again, but not so heavy as it had been before, and with a more definite wriggling that could only have been produced by the movement of tail and fins. I increased the speed of wind. Unconscious of its peril the fish was actually swimming upwards, moving with foolish obedience to the pull on the line, like a dog on a leash.

But was it so foolish? Already I was seeing

myself abandoning my fishing trip (for even catching one of Bill Haley's big pollack would be an anti-climax after this), hauling *Amanda's* anchor, moving at top speed in to the Town Quay, where Bill himself might be among the curious spectators, then carrying my fish—and I might even need some help—to Percy Varcoe's fishmonger's shop, to have it weighed and admired.

My eyes were on the ascending line. I was waiting for the first glimpse of my quarry through the murky water but out of the tail of my eye I saw that my gaff was within hand's reach. And then it happened, I was winding steadily. There came one terrific tug, the rod bent until its tip was in the water, then sprang up again. I reeled in, saw my sinker, and the brass swivel. But the trace and the hook and the fish had gone.

What was that fish? It *might* have been a bass, behaving unconventionally, a pollack, a skate, a halibut (occasionally big halibut have been caught by the local river salmon netters), a conger, ling—any species listed in the catalogue of British fish known to grow to a prodigious size. It just *might* have been that rarest of all British fish, the Royal sturgeon, in which case I would have had the honour of sending it to Her Majesty the Queen.

I shall never know. It was my biggest fish that got away.

2

FOWEY with its harbour and tidal creeks and entrancing coastal coves may be an angler's El Dorado, as well as an agreeable place to live in: yet my mind is rarely free of that red-roofed village on the north-east Yorkshire coast known as Robin Hood's Bay, which with a writer's licence I have re-named Bramblewick, where I spent my childhood and youth and much of my adult life, 'attached', 'unattached' and 'semi-detached'.

Without the stimulus of Huxley's[1] mescalin, or Rich Ward's[2] lysergic acid, drugs which unravel the tight coils of memory and the sub-conscious mind, I can transport myself into the past so that the past becomes the present. I never dig for worms in the mud of one of Fowey's creeks but I am back, a bare-footed lad, on the patchy sandbank of Bramblewick's Landing at low tide, picking up the worms as old Captain Bunny forks them out, in the hope that he'll take me fishing when the tide flows. I never make an eye-splice in one of *Amanda's* ropes but what I am back in the Lunns' boats watching Marney Lunn's more skilful fingers doing the same with a lobster pot tow. When I hear the exploding maroons summoning Fowey's motor lifeboat crew to a mission—and it's usually in summer, to a capsized yacht or canoe—I am back in Bramblewick

[1] *Doors of Perception* – Aldous Huxley

[2] *A Drug Taker's Notes* – R.H. Ward

on a stormy winter's night hearing the sound of heavy seabooted feet hurrying down the cobbled street to the Dock and the lifeboat house, and shouts of *'there's a ship ashore—there's a ship ashore!'*

There are no all-time fishermen in Bramblewick now, as indeed there is none in Fowey, for even Bill Haley, who makes his living from the sporting visitors, lays up his boat for most of the winter months. But when I was a lad there were more than a score of fishermen working the whole year round: long lining in winter, crabbing and lobstering in spring, and these would be joined by several more for the summer salmon-netting season.

Their craft were cobles, some of them thirty feet in length with an eight-foot beam amidship tapering to a narrow high-flaired bow with a deep keel and a low stern with undercut transom, and in beaching they were brought in stern first, the lean bow giving little resistance to the surf. They were clinker built, with wide overlapping planks or strakes, beautifully moulded. These were painted in contrasting colours.

They were all in those days pulling or sailing boats. They were equipped with broad rudders reaching well below the hull which functioned as an extra keel enabling them to sail close to the wind. The sail was a dipping lug whose yard had to be moved round the mast at change of tack. But they had to carry ballast, sandstone blocks tied with short ropes or strops to a longer rope with a buoy on one end so that all could be dropped overboard when landing and picked up before setting out next day for the fishing grounds.

Even without the ballast, the cobles were very heavy, and always in winter time they had to be hauled up to the safety of the Dock.

It was exciting to watch them come in when they

were long lining, and with luck this would happen at dinner time when school was closed or better still on a Saturday. I'd hurry through my meal and dash down to the beach. The men would have set off in the dark, long before daybreak. They liked to get back when the tide had ebbed from the slipway foot and from the shore end of the East Scaur, the shale reef which with the West Scaur formed the Landing. This would mean that they wouldn't have so far to carry their catch and gear and haul up the cobles.

I can see it now as I write: a grey day in November, the sky overcast, no wind so that the men have been unable to use their sails, although they have taken their ballast 'in case'; the sea calm but with a gentle swell baring its teeth on the scaur ends, a good day for fishing except for the extra labour at the oars, pulling to and back from the grounds.

There are six cobles, each with a sentimental or religious propitiatory name: *Two Sisters, The Brothers, The Friend, Harvest Home, Gratitude, Providence,* three men in each. They are all, except Oliver, youngest of the predominant Fosdyck family and 'young' Matt, son of old Matt Cooper, coxwain of the lifeboat, middle-aged or elderly, and bearded; old Matt with such a tangle of grizzly grey hair on his face that only his nose and eyes and an inch or two of his forehead under the brim of his hard felt hat are visible. They have taken off their oilskins. They are wearing guernseys, with sleeves rolled up, showing the thick muscles of their arms. Their leather seaboots come up to their thighs. They are big strong men.

Having dumped their ballast, the cobles are pulled in to shallow water until they ground. Some of the men climb overboard, while others pack the fish into big two-handled baskets, which are now carried ashore.

Carved out of the shale of the scaur are several cavities, filled with water left by the tide. The fish are dumped alongside them. The men wade out for another load. Mostly the fish are codling, white bellied with dark green-brown speckled backs, but if they have been caught among the tangles close in they are almost brown as the weed and these are called sprags. There are billet, which are half-grown coal fish, but when very small, pennocks, which in summer we lads catch ourselves, fishing from the scaurs. There are ling, and whiting pout, and, if the fishers have been lucky, haddock with the finger marks close to their heads which were supposed to show that these were the fish caught by St. Peter in the Sea of Galilee, although of course the haddock is a salt-water fish. None of the first fish brought ashore is very big, but even the smallest excite my envy, and when I see some of the men wading in, carrying in each hand a cod so big that its tail trails in the water I am thinking that of all the occupations none can be more exciting than the fishermen's.

With sharp knives, the fish are slit open, revealing their entrails: the short gullet, the distended stomach, the enormous liver with its little sac of emerald bile, the intestines, the roe, or milt, according to sex. All this is ripped out, the carcases flung into the pool to be washed, then carried up to the sheds to be packed for market.

The screaming gulls which since the coming in of the cobles have been wheeling overhead swoop down for the offal, but we lads dispute it with them for the first pickings. We don't want the strong-smelling and oily and stronger-tasting livers, but the roes and milt are prize titbits to be taken home to our mothers for cooking; and some of us take a not completely morbid interest in squeezing out the contents of the stomach of those big cod to discover what they had eaten before they were trapped by the fisherman's bait: crabs, small lobsters, anemones, other fish of various sorts, all except the one nearest the gullet semi-digested, not to be taken home with the roes and the milt, but yielding valuable information to a would-be angler. Besides, according to what we have heard, strange things are sometimes found in the stomachs of big fish which must have been swallowed by mistake: silver coins, a brooch which might have come from a drowned woman, a dental plate with gold teeth. This was supposed to have belonged to a summer visitor who had been seasick while fishing at the whiting grounds.

Each coble has its launching carriage, a thick oak axle with a pair of small stout wagon wheels. It takes all the men to lift each coble, one at a time on to its carriage, bow first, and then eased on until it is balanced when it is made fast with ropes to the thole pins. Then we all take hold of the long hawsers, and away we go, shouting, 'Heave—ho, Heave—ho!' to the slipway foot, and then more slowly up the steep slipway to the Dock, to be safely berthed for the night. . .

This has been one of the fishermen's lucky days. Just as clearly I can recall another winter's morning. We are all on our way to school, the detested bell ringing in our ears, when we hear the double bang of the lifeboat gun.

We know we'll be punished, but we rush down to the dock, thinking (and even hoping) that we'll see a ship on the rocks, and the lifeboat being launched to the rescue of its crew. The doors of the lifeboat house are shut however. From the talk of the old men and women who have gathered at the slipway top, and with our own eyes, we soon know what has happened. It's the fishermen themselves, including the coxwain and the lifeboat crew, who are in danger. The gun has been fired only to let everyone in the village know.

With an offshore wind the cobles have sailed swiftly to the fishing grounds, well out in the bay. Before they have had time to haul their lines, the wind has veered to north-east and is rising to a gale. With reefed sails all six cobles are beating for the Landing. . . It is now low tide. The water in the Landing between the scaurs is still calm, but big waves are already breaking on the sunken scaur ends, and even far out where there are no rocks the waves are topped with foam.

We all know that in the past several fishermen have lost their lives through their cobles capsizing when trying to get through the Landing mouth with a rough sea. The women, especially those whose relations are now in danger, look very anxious. The old retired fishermen, and some of them are more than eighty years of age, don't just stand and stare. They have started to take the launching carriages down to the beach, for the tide is on the turn. It will flow very fast with the gale behind it and make more difficult and dangerous the job of getting the cobles up on to the Dock, even if they do get ashore safely.

The school bell has stopped ringing. That doesn't bother us at present. We help with the carriages, all the time looking at the cobles. They are sailing very fast, heeling over with the wind and sometimes almost disappearing in the hollows between the waves, then rising so that we can see the fore part of their keels. The wind is bitterly cold. There are flakes of snow, blowing about like little feathers. And just beyond the headland at the north end of the Bay there is a dark cloud, with what looks like a solid grey wall falling from it to the sea: it is a squall, driving quickly shorewards.

Will it beat the cobles? Two of them are close together and not more than a few hundred yards from the posts that mark the Landing mouth across which the waves are now starting to break. The others are strung seawards behind them, old Matt Cooper's coble last of all. The first two lower their sails, turn about, and with their oars start to back in. A big wave rises as they near the posts. They pull ahead as it curls over to break. It lifts the cobles almost on end, then as it passes, they back with all their strength in its wake. Another wave follows. Again they pull ahead. Again they back, and now they are inside the posts and before the next wave rushes in they are safe in unbroken water.

But as the third coble draws near the posts and lowers its sail, the squall breaks and everything seaward is blotted out by a downpour of driving hailstones. The wind is so strong that we can hardly stand. It lashes even the smooth water of the Landing. It balloons the furled sail of one of the grounded cobles and the men have to hang on to it. We can't see the posts. Then suddenly we hear a shout and through the murk of spume and hailstones and churned-up water we see the shape of the third coble moving in. There is no sign of the other three.

If those of us on shore cannot see the posts, it will be just as hard for those coming in, although the hail won't be driving in their faces. If they can't see the posts and get on the wrong side either of the East or

West Scaur they'll be driven aground among the breakers, and smash up for certain. Yet there is nothing the men ashore can do to help, and already with the old men and the coastguards they are starting to get the grounded cobles on to their carriages; for the tide is flowing very fast.

Then, although the wind is as strong as ever, the hailstones, which have turned the scaurs white, stop. The mist clears, leaving a patch of blue sky overhead. We can see the whole of the Bay, torn with breakers and with another dark squall driving in from the north. And there, just outside the landing posts, are the three cobles, old Matt's with a broken mast and sail flapping over its side; the men in them pulling ahead into the waves, now bigger than ever.

But their chance has come. A big wave rolls in. They pull hard into it. It curls over and breaks, and like the first cobles to come in, they back in its wake, then pull again to meet the next which is the biggest of all and breaking from post to post. For a moment it looks as though it has overwhelmed them, for they disappear from sight. Then we see them again, one coble almost broadside on, but with strong strokes of the oars they slew it fair in time to meet the next wave. They back again in its seething wake as it passes, and before another wave rolls in they are inside the posts in the lee of the West Scaur, throwing their ballast overboard before grounding.

None of the men looks as though they have been frightened, and have just escaped from death. Only old Matt, who has lost his hat as well as the mast of his coble, looks bothered. He is rubbing the top of his head, which is completely bald, and must be sore from the hailstones pelting on it. They have no fish to land. They have saved their lives and their boats, but it will be days and it may be weeks before the sea is calm enough for them to go out to haul their lines, and very likely the buoys that mark them have been washed away so that they may not find them at all.

Another squall has broken, only this time it is driving snow instead of hail, a blizzard. We lads too—redundant to the job of hauling up the cobles with so many adult helpers—have our own Landing to negotiate, in the shape of an irate, implacable schoolmaster. But as we run up to the village (water squelching in our boots) to meet our fate, I am still thinking that when I grow up I want to be a fisherman.

3

OF course, the season we liked best was summer, especially when the holidays came and the weather was fine with the sun shining all day long, and the sea calm and the water warm so that all you needed to wear was a shirt and short trousers with sand shoes on your feet to protect them from the sharp-pointed barnacles that encrusted the scaurs. It didn't matter if you got your sand shoes wet.

The fishermen were happier in summer too for they could keep their cobles moored in the Landing, and only haul them to the Dock if there was a storm. Salmoning wasn't such hard work either, for all they had to do was shoot and haul their nets. But as they did this at night, setting off at dusk and landing again at daybreak, we never saw what they caught. The salmon and salmon trout were never gutted like the other fish but packed in boxes and sent off to market from the railway station, but the fishermen got as much as a shilling a pound for them, and only tuppence for cod and often less.

Although I thought they were very brave, especially when they went out in the lifeboat to a wreck no matter how stormy the weather, I didn't really like any of the coblemen. They'd never say 'thank you' when you helped them haul up. They only let you have the cod roes because they didn't want them themselves. They got angry if you dared to climb inside their cobles even when they were in the Dock and would shout at you gruffly. They would never dream of letting any boy go out with them even in fine weather.

In summer, however, when the visitors came to stay in the village, there were several old men who made money by taking them out in their small rowing boats. They were charged sixpence an hour, just for a row, a shilling an hour if they were taken fishing to the whiting grounds. These old men were not real fishermen, but retired sailors, and among them was Captain Bunny, who had a rowing boat called *Lydia.* This had been the ship's boat of a schooner of the same name, which had been wrecked on the coast of Norfolk.

These pleasure boatmen had 'boys' whose job it was to keep the boat afloat when the tide was ebbing so that the boatmen could stand on the slipway as the visitors walked down to the beach and ask them if they wanted a pull or to go fishing. If the 'boy' was lucky his master would let him go in the boat to help to pull, or if it was a fishing trip, to bait the lines for the customers.

I had learned how to pull a boat, and there was nothing I would have liked better than a job like this. Whenever I saw one of the old men digging worms I would go and help, but usually there would be other boys doing the same thing, and as the 'boys' who had the jobs often got a tip from the customers, I didn't see much chance of being taken on especially by Captain Bunny, the one I liked best. His 'boy' was his nephew, Garney, whose father was captain of a collier sailing ship trading between Newcastle and London, sometimes Holland and Denmark. Garney himself would go to sea when he was old enough to leave school. Once or twice he had let me go in *Lydia* when he was keeping it afloat and even let me pull.

But if I couldn't go fishing in a boat there was

always pennocking. One of the best times for this was when the flowing tide had reached the Rocket Post Scaur. This was quite close to the village and the East Scaur of the Landing. It got its name because there was a thick, high wooden post cemented into a hole in the shale. It had steps fastened to it almost to the top, and it was used to represent the mast of a stranded ship for the coastguards to practise life-saving rocket apparatus rill.

The scaur was high on one side and sloped away on the other. It also sloped towards the shore so that when the tide flowed it made a sort of island which got smaller and smaller as the water rose around it and the bottom of the post. You could stay on it until it was up to your ankles, when it would be just over your knees for wading ashore.

One day six of us were pennocking on the scaur, five locals counting me, and one visitor boy. This boy had a real fishing rod with a reel and a very thin line and a painted float. He also had a basket round his shoulder to hold his fish when he caught them. The rest of us had hazel sticks with lengths of grocer's string for lines, and ha'penny hooks with catgut snoods. For floats we had bottle corks. As we knew all about pennocking we naturally thought we'd show this visitor boy with his swanky rod how to catch them, although he was using the same bait, the soft part of limpets.

The weather was just right. The sea was smooth. The sun was shining. The water warm and clear. We stood close together on the high edge of the scaur, which really formed a cliff five feet down into the water. The bottom was level shale with some clumps of bladder wrack which floated straight up as the water rose, and by the time it was halfway up the 'cliff' the pennocks started coming in.

Pennocks don't swim in shoals like sand eels or sprats which are all the same size and keep close together. There are big ones and little ones and they dart in all directions looking for food. The big ones are about six inches long, the little ones not much bigger than shrimps, but they are cheeky and often snatch your bait before the big ones chase them away.

The visitor boy was on the edge of the scaur farthest from the beach. To my surprise he was the first to catch a fish, a big one too, and he'd got another before we started getting them. I wasn't really jealous, for I caught one that was bigger than his, and soon we were all catching fish as fast as we could bait our hooks.

But while we fished the tide was flowing, the water rising up the cliff. Already the scaur was an island. Soon it would be lapping over the highest part and we'd have to wade ashore. And then an extraordinary thing happened. In between the clumps of bladder wrack, now completely underwater, there appeared a huge dark-green eel, moving just like a snake. It was on the bottom, but it saw our baits and swam upwards. I saw it open its mouth and snap the bait of the visitor boy. He gave a shout. The rod bent and cracked. His line broke. The eel with the line and the float trailing from its mouth went for the next bait belonging to the boy beside me. His line broke too, just as though it had been sliced with a knife. My bait was only a few inches away. The eel snapped at it. My hook was in its mouth. I gave a gentle tug as it moved to the next bait, and as it snapped this it turned downwards with a swish of its tail, breaking both lines as though they had been cotton. It disappeared among the weeds.

The visitor boy was crying as he looked at his broken rod. I felt like crying too when I thought how wonderful it would have been if I had caught it. Then I remembered that I had in my pocket a piece of real fishermen's line with a cod hook I'd found on the beach one day. The hook would have been too big for pennocks. I was so excited that I got it in a tangle and by the time I had cleared it and tied it to my rod there was no dry scaur left. The water was over my ankles. The other lads had waded ashore. I didn't mind if the water was up to my waist. If there was one eel like that big one there might be another, and I wasn't going to miss a chance of catching it for fear of getting my breeches wet!

I put two limpets on the hook. I didn't bother about a float. But thinking the rod might break I had knotted the line at its tip and left enough spare line to reach down the rod to my hand and loop it round my wrist. I cast the bait out as far as it would go, and before it sank to the bottom I saw not another eel, but the same one with the visitor boy's float still trailing from its mouth. It was swimming for my bait. It opened its mouth, snapped it, and I knew it was hooked, for it was pulling like mad, twisting and turning so that I could see its white belly, trying to get off. It pulled so strong that if I hadn't looped the end of the line round my wrist I couldn't have held it. It was trying to pull seawards. With the water all round me and well above my ankles I knew it was no good trying to haul it on the scaur. The only thing to do was to wade ashore along the scaur dragging it with me, and then to haul it up the dry beach where the other lads were now waiting and watching me. They must have seen that I had hooked something, and one of them shouted:

'Eh—t' water's got deep. If you don't come soon you'll be drowned!'

I started pulling at the line, instead of just holding on. The fish came in a bit, and then suddenly it made a rush and came past me so that the line went slack, and it darted round the bottom of the rocket post which was about six feet from the scaur edge and in deeper water. The line caught on the post. The fish came back towards me, and again went round. But the line hadn't broken. I still held the end of it although it was slack. I waded to the post. The water was over my knees, level with the first step, and I climbed on to it out of the water, and tried to disentangle the line. I was too excited to notice a boat coming towards me, until I heard a shout:

'Eh, what are you at? Don't you know t' tide's coming in, you daft beggar?'

It was Captain Bunny, in the *Lydia,* and he pulled almost up to the post.

'I've got a big fish,' I shouted. 'My line has caught round the post. Can you help me unloosen it?'

He pulled in closer, shipped his oars, and looking down saw the eel.

'Well, I'm danged!' he said. 'It's a conger. Where's your line? Have you got the end of it?'

'Yes.'

'Then hold on to it, don't try and haul in. Here get on board.'

I got into the *Lydia,* the end of the line still round my wrist. The Captain took it from me. Then he got hold of a gaff (a stout shaft with a hook lashed to one end), leaned over the side and after several tries jabbed the hook into the fish. He moved it round the post so that the line was clear and handed the line back to me.

'Now you can haul in,' he said. 'It's your fish—not mine!'

I hauled in, the Captain taking part of the weight with his gaff. It was safe inside the boat, wriggling on the bottom boards, snapping like a mad dog, until the Captain gave it a whack on its head with a mallet and stunned it, although it still went on wriggling.

'Well, I'm danged!' he said then. 'Fancy catching a conger like that off the scaur. But you might have got drowned, you young beggar. It's a good job I had the boat afloat, waiting to take a party out fishing.'

'Yes, it was, Captain. Thank you very much for helping me. I couldn't have caught it without you. Shall I pull back for you?'

'Can you pull a boat?' he said.

I took the oars. They were a bit heavy but I managed them all right. I could see the Captain, who had sat down in the stern, was pleased, and I dared to say to him:

'Will Garney be going off with you fishing?'

'Nay. Garney's gone to off to Newcastle. He's going for a voyage on his father's ship.'

We were getting near the slipway, and again I dared to say:

'I can keep your boat afloat for you, Captain, if you like, until you're ready to go off fishing. I wouldn't mind going fishing either,' I added. 'I've never been fishing in a boat.'

The Captain laughed.

'You're a corker, you are. I'll think about it. You get your ways home with your fish, and ask your mother if you can go, and get some more clothes to put on, and hurry back sharp. If the folks who are going haven't come by that time, maybe I will, maybe I will. I can see you're a good hand at pulling.'

4

FOR that summer, and the next, I was Captain Bunny's regular 'boy'. On his first voyage on his father's ship, Garney fell down the hold and broke his leg, and came home on crutches. By next year he was old enough to leave school, and as his leg had mended he joined the ship as cabin boy.

The Captain paid me a penny a week wages. I also got a few tips from our customers. My job, apart from keeping the *Lydia* afloat while the Captain watched out on the slipway or went home for his dinner, was to keep the boat clean and tidy, inside and out, get bait, to help him pull close in along the shore if it was just a sixpence an hour pleasure trip, or out to the whiting grounds for fishing. If there were ladies with us when we were fishing, I would have to bait their lines, but unless the boat was crowded, the Captain would always let me fish too.

Although he had no teeth and was clean shaven, I thought that the Captain was almost exactly like the pictures I had seen of Father Christmas. The hair on his head was snow white, his cheeks were round, he had twinkling blue eyes and he was always smiling and good tempered, even when, at the whiting grounds, the fish were not biting, when he would say, and it would never fail to make me laugh:

'Plain coffee—plain coffee!'

But usually they did bite. The whiting grounds were about three-quarters of a mile straight out from the Landing, and about the same distance from the high cliff which formed the north end of the Bay. The railway line to Whitby ran close to the edge of this cliff, and you knew you were on the ground when a railway embankment was in sight through a hollow in the cliff, and the chimneys of the cottages of the old coastguard station were in line with the watchhouse. Once there, the anchor would be dropped (even at high tide of springs there were only five fathoms of water), the lines baited and fishing would start.

They were handlines, unwound from square wood frames which the Captain had made himself, and kept in a box when dry and not in use. The two hooks on short, thin, but strong, snoods were attached to a device like the beam of a grocer's scales, and called a chopstick. It was a thin iron or brass rod looped at each end for the snoods, and with a lead cone in the middle to which the handline was knotted. When baited you lowered it down until it hit the bottom. Then you raised it enough to keep the bait clear of the crabs (eating, not shore crabs) but not too high for flatfish.

It was real fishing this, and terribly exciting when you felt the first nibble. You waited a bit, then if the nibbling went on you gave the line a jerk, and if you still felt the fish you hauled in as fast as you could, being careful not to get the coils of the line tangled. And you never knew until the fish was almost up to the boat what sort it was, for even on the calmest day the water was never really clear because of the muddy bottom.

There were plaice and dabs, flounders and sometimes soles. With flatfish, which don't go in shoals, usually we had to wait some time between bites. It was different when the whiting were 'in'. Then we would be hauling them two at a time, and there would be two more on before the chopsticks had got down to the bottom. This would mean that the tin of bait would soon be empty, even though we were making four baits out of one worm by cutting it up. That wouldn't matter with whiting, for they were cannibals, and we'd cut one into pieces and use these for bait.

We never caught cod or billet although this was one of the grounds where the coble men shot their long lines in winter. But they never caught flatfish or whiting. Every sort of fish seemed to have its own special feeding grounds according to the time of year. Yet often when the whiting were biting we'd get a grey gurnard, a fish with sharp spines on its head and fins, which had to be taken very carefully from the hook. They had to be skinned before they were ready for cooking, but it was worth the trouble for they tasted even better than plaice or sole.

Sometimes instead of whiting we'd get nothing but haddock. Sometimes, although usually they were caught trolling with a spinner, we'd be hauling mackerel two at a time, and getting no whiting at all. And sometimes when we'd got the box nearly full we'd start getting dog fish, which are small sharks so fierce that they drive the other fish away, and, although they pulled hard and were supposed to be no good to eat, this usually meant hauling up the anchor and pulling for home.

Although the customers only paid a shilling an hour they expected to take as many of the fish as they wanted. Of course they would pick out the plaice if there were any, and we'd have to gut them and put them on string so that they could walk up the village to the lodgings for everyone to see. But whether they gave me a tip or not, when there were fish left over the Captain always gave me as many as I could carry to take home, and as the customers wouldn't know how to skin gurnard, and how delicious they were, I could take some of these too.

All this, and the memory of my happiest of adventures with the Captain in the *Lydia,* which will be related in due course, was vividly in my mind one day in the early summer of 1964, when alone and in our dinghy, I was pulling straight out to sea from Fowey's harbour. I was alone because my family had gone to Deal to stay with my wife's parents. I was in the dinghy because *Amanda* was neaped on the beach, drying out for scraping and painting. I was bound at last for Fowey's own whiting grounds.

5

I HAD no plan when I set out on that trip for anything more ambitious than trolling for pollack outside the harbour mouth. The estuary bass had come, and temporarily gone, where to, only Bill Haley, and the other experts with their big high-powered, semi-cabin cruisers, would know.

Three of these craft, Bill's included, were equipped with echo sounders. The bass and big pollack, when they are not feeding on sand eels, favour rocky ground, prominences which rise like little hills from the level, deep sea-bed but are invisible from the surface. The echo sounder, which has replaced the sounding lead on all modern vessels, can accurately produce on a moving paper graph the contours, the 'hills' and 'valleys' of the sea-bed. It can, if the shoals are dense enough, spot and measure concentrations of herring, pilchard and other fish and is of immense value to commercial fishermen. As the summer-paying anglers want and expect to catch the big fish, the boats which are equipped with this cunning apparatus never lack clients.

Although I would observe the return of these boats to the Town Quay, the landing of their catch, with envy, I had no yearnings for a bigger boat than *Amanda,* let alone an echo sounder, even if I could have afforded the cost. I was normally content with the fish and the fishing that came my way in the hours of leisure dictated by my conscience as a married man with a living to earn.

But on this day (it was afternoon, and a reasonable amount of duty work had been done) I was aware of a discontent which increased as I started fishing outside the harbour mouth and at once hooked a bream (known locally as shad), not more than three inches long. I unhooked it and threw it back, baited again and immediately hooked another the same size. I hesitated about putting on another bait. My supply of rag worms was not big, and if I went on like this it would be exhausted before I had a chance at a pollack.

Shad come in to the Fowey coast without fail every summer. They are pretty fish, shaped like a perch, and like a gurnard, armed with needle-sharp spines. Like a gurnard, too, their flesh is white, firm and delicious to eat, but they've got to be expertly skinned. They are voracious feeders and as they come in big shoals, can be relied upon to provide sport for the not-too-particular summer visitors. Although never more than half a pound in weight, they are usually a respectable size. The two I had caught and put back were babies. I tried another bait. Up came another identical in size. No wonder that I should start thinking of my native village, of Captain Bunny, the *Lydia* and the whiting ground, with its fat plaice, dabs, sole, gurnard, haddock, mackerel, as well as whiting!

There was, I had been assured by many of the locals, including Bill Haley, a whiting ground at Fowey. It was about three and a half miles seawards from the harbour mouth. It was a wide stretch of level ground with a shingly bottom, and easy to find in clear weather. There was a white wooden cross fixed on a rock at the Polruan side of the harbour mouth. Moving seawards you kept this cross in a line with a big house on the Fowey side which had a conspicious red roof, and you went on until on the easterly coastline you saw an old coastguard watchhouse visible beyond a rocky headland called Pencarrow.

Bill had sounded rather contemptuous about it. Flatfish, whiting, gurnard, were not in his line. You never got bass or pollack there. Others had warned me that it was no good except in calm weather with a neap tide, for the tidal current ran very strong. Although it was only three and a half miles from the Fowey coastline, you were another three miles from the shores of St. Austell Bay and an off shore wind scarcely noticeable at Fowey could quickly raise a nasty sea. You needed a big motor boat, at least thirty fathoms of stout rope and a heavy anchor to fish there in comfort and safety, and at the first sign of a rising wind you had to make for home.

Possibly for this reason I had never ventured it. I have a great respect for the sea. *Amanda's* original engine had been a converted vintage Austin Seven, with a reversible propeller. It served me faithfully in several emergencies and on its final trip up-river to Golant, where I was to have it overhauled by an engineer, it had run with a cracked and leaking cylinder and its sump full of sea-water. This was the end and I had replaced it with a brand new Stuart Turner Four.

I was now in the dinghy, however. *Amanda* was beached. Yet it was a lovely day, a cloudless sky, no wind, the sea dead smooth, visibility perfect. The tides were neap. It would have been ideal for one of our bathing picnics and I could only hope that my family were enjoying the same weather on the Kentish coast, thereby stilling my last twinge of conscience. I wound in my trolling line and changed the hook for a mackerel spinner, for a mackerel would be an even better bait than worm for bottom fishing. At a good pace I pulled seawards, with the wooden mark (it was called Punch Cross) in line with the red-roofed house.

It was too early in the season yet for the sea to be crowded with pleasure boats, but a long way eastwards towards Polperro I could see several of the local 'bass' fishers, and I guessed that Bill would be among them. They were too far off for me to be sure. There were no craft ahead of me. It looked as though I would have the whiting grounds to myself.

Would it prove as prolific as the Bramblewick ground? Or would it, in Captain Bunny's well remembered phrase be 'plain coffee'? Generally speaking, the farther out you went from the coast and the deeper the water, the bigger and more varied in species the fish. With two of us pulling in the *Lydia* we could reach the Bramblewick grounds in twenty minutes. I reckoned it was going to take me at least an hour to reach my present destination. Although I could see Pencarrow Head, jutting out from the line of cliffs a mile east of Polruan and dividing Lantic Bay from Lantivet Bay, after half an hour's pulling, the old coastguard watchhouse was still invisible.

I should have no difficulty in recognising it. Years ago, when Sir Gerald du Maurier was still alive and his daughter Daphne, with two novels already to her credit, had romantically met and married 'Tommy' (the late Lieut.-General Sir Frederick Browning), she had taken a lease of the watchhouse, not God forbid, as a matrimonial home but as a place where she could write when he was absent on his military duties. It was little more than a miniature two-roomed cottage built at the edge of the cliff, with steps leading down to a cove. It had been unoccupied for many years and was dilapidated. There was no road to it and, as no local builder would take it on, Daphne gave me the job of making it habitable, with timber and cement all sea-borne and landed in the cove from Tommy's motor launch. There, before she and her husband went to live in the mansion of Menabilly (the 'Manderley' of the book), she found the inspiration for her most famous novel *Rebecca.*

The dinghy was an easy boat to pull, and with my muscles hardened with long use my progress over the calm sea was effortless. Punch Cross, although gradually looking smaller was still easily visible. To the west above Gribben Head the crests of the conical china-clay tips inland from St. Austell were coming in sight, gleaming white in the sun, like snow-clad mountains.

My rod leaning over the stern suddenly jerked, the reel against the check whizzed round. I shipped the oars, seized the rod and got the weight of a fish. It felt like a mackerel. There was no need to play it. I reeled in until it came in sight, zigzagging, leaping out of the water, not a mackerel but a gar fish, known by some anglers as a stink fish.

Normally if I catch a gar fish I unhook and let it go. It is an extraordinary-looking creature, with a long thin cylindrical body, deep blue-green on top, merging into an iridescent silver belly. Its eyes are large and the head tapers into a long beak, more like a bird's than a fish's. It is built for speed and is certainly faster than a mackerel. Its bones are green. But the most striking thing about it is its smell, which hits you like a gas when you lift it on board, the concentrated smell of cod-liver oil, a smell that is sublimated into taste if you have the courage to eat its cooked flesh.

But I needed a fish to cut up for bait. As there was no indication of a shoal of mackerel on the placid sea—no feeding gulls or gannets—I kept it, thinking that its smell might prove an added attraction. I put the spinner overboard again and went on pulling, my excitement mounting. It couldn't be long now before the watchhouse came in sight and I could make a start. Often in the *Lydia* the fish had started biting the first moment our lines had gone over, with the anchor just down.

Then something happened that temporarily put both past and present whiting grounds from my mind. About two hundred yards westerly of my course several dark triangular objects had appeared on the surface of the water. At first I took them to be the dorsal fins of a school of dolphins. They were scarcely moving however. Like whales, dolphins come to the surface to 'breathe' and dive immediately. These fins, I was soon certain, were those of basking sharks, creatures I had never seen alive except in films like Flaherty's *Man of Aran,* although I had been told that they were frequent visitors to the Cornish coast in summer.

I pulled slowly, stealthily towards them. Basking sharks I knew were harmless, except when attacked. They have a commercial value, their huge livers being rich in oil, and are caught with harpoon on the west coasts of Scotland and Ireland, the danger being in their tail, which, lashing, could smash a small boat to pieces. But like the whale-bone whales, they have no teeth and they feed exclusively on plankton, the minute creatures and 'plants' which exist near the surface of the sea in profusion, which they extract through their sieve-like gills.

They were moving very slowly. There were five

of them. I got near enough to one to see its whole length from snout to tail, and it must have measured at least twice the length of the dinghy. I stopped pulling at that respectful distance and watched it with great interest, wishing only that I was in *Amanda* so that from her deck I could have had a still better view. Then, satisfied that I had at last seen a basking shark, I turned and pulled back to my course, with Punch Cross and the red-roofed house in line and certainly, three miles distant but the watchhouse still invisible. I should have another half mile to go.

But shortly I stopped again, and it might have been intuition. Apart from the diversion of the sharks, I had been concentrating my attention on the shoreward view. Now I looked ahead and I saw, extending along the horizon, dividing sea from the blue sky a narrow, even streak of what undoubtedly was mist and what might be fog. I looked shorewards. From west to east, from the Dodman to distant Rame Head where the coastline recedes to Plymouth Sound: inland to Bodmin Moor and the china-clay tips of St. Austell, all was clear in the summer sun. I could see the 'bass boats' well out to sea to westward of me. Above, there was not a cloud in the sky. Yet looking ahead once more I saw that the streak had thickened, that the horizon line was blurred, and I felt on my face a movement of cool air, scarcely a wind, yet definitely landwards in direction.

Resting on my oars I waited apprehensively. I hadn't long to wait. The movement of air became a gentle but definite wind, enough to furr the surface of the water. First with it came wisps of slowly twirling diaphanous mist between which the blue sky was still visible. Then came the fog, allowing me one last glimpse of the sun and sky and the coast before it blotted them out completely.

If there is one thing I have learned in the course of my life-long devotion to fishing it is to take 'the slings and arrows of outrageous fortune' philosophically. Here I was within a few more minutes pulling off what might have proved a most exciting climax to my expedition, as exciting perhaps even as any I'd had with Captain Bunny, faced indeed with a stroke of outrageous fortune. So near and yet so far, for although I'd had that last glimpse of the coastline, I hadn't seen the watchhouse, and already looking around me, I couldn't tell now in which direction the coast lay, for the wind which might have given me a clue had dropped, as though its sole purpose had been to envelop me in this bank of fog.

It was not a pea-soup fog. There was an area of visibility around me of at least a hundred yards. I could have seen the basking sharks if they had decided to swim in my direction, and taken avoiding action. But otherwise it would be imprudent for me to move at all, for I had no compass. I decided to take a chance with the sharks; to drop the anchor and stay where I was in the hope that the fog would lift, as it was bound to do eventually. Fortunately I had an ample length of rope.

There was not much of it left when the anchor touched the bottom, supporting evidence that I was not so far from the grounds. I wound in my line, changed the spinner for a three-hook paternoster and a four-ounce sinker, a tackle which, with no disrespect to the memory of Captain Bunny, was a more efficient one than his chopsticks. I put a worm on the bottom hook and pieces of the odoriferous gar fish on the other two, let it go down to the bottom. I moved from the pulling thwart to the stern seat which was more comfortable, and with the rod butt within reach and its tip projecting over the gunwale, lit a cigarette.

My eyes were on the rod tip of course, and ever optimistic I started to picture what might be happening down below; a huge plaice sniffing at the worm on the bottom hook, making up its mind, a shoal of whiting, swimming baitwards lured by the smell of gar fish.

But the rod tip gave no responding jerk. When I had finished my cigarette I hauled in, found all three baits intact. I let them go again and resumed my vigil. The minutes passed. I hauled again. Still no sign of fish. It looked like 'plain coffee'. But for the fog, I would have hauled up the anchor and tried another place. The fog, however, showed no sign of clearing. The calm continued, and I began to feel worried, for although a summer fog in otherwise fine weather usually clears soon it was not inevitable that it would. It might last into the night.

I gave up winding in my line up and down just to look at those unwanted baits. I was getting hungry too, and for once on a fishing trip bored. I would have welcomed a sight of those basking sharks, if only to relieve the monotonous aspect of the surrounding fog and the grey calm water. I was tempted to haul up the anchor and start pulling, taking a chance of going in the right direction for the shore, or at least a place where there were fish. And then, it must have been nearly an hour since the fog had descended on me, I heard the sound of a motor.

I stood up and shouted as loud as I could: 'Ahoy—ahoy!'

There was no answer, but the sound of the motor grew stronger. I shouted again. This time I heard voices: and there appeared through the curtain of fog a boat coming towards me. I shouted more anxiously. It looked as though it was going to run me down. It swerved, and, almost alongside me, reversed engine, and came to a stop. It was Bill Haley.

For a moment neither of us spoke. I'd had a fright, and Bill must have had one too, but he recovered first.

'What the hell are you doing here? I nearly barged into you.'

'I was making for the whiting grounds when the fog came. I dropped anchor, hoping it might lift, and I've been trying to get a fish while waiting.'

Bill, who had been a petty officer in the Navy before retirement, never pulled his punches.

'You ought to have had more sense coming out here in a dinghy. This fog's not going to lift without an offshore breeze. Haven't you got a compass?'

He had two well-to-do passengers with him, who were eyeing me with some amusement.

'No, Bill,' I said. 'Mine's on *Amanda* and *Amanda's* on the beach waiting to dry out for painting. It was fine enough when I set out.'

'How many fish have you got ? You're not on the whiting grounds here. You've got to be a quarter of a mile to sout'ard.'

Ironically I held up what remained of my gar fish. 'That's all I've got. The fog came on before I sighted the old watchhouse.'

I guessed what was coming, and I had to ask the painful question:

'How have *you* done?'

Bill bent down and lifted up an enormous pollack. One of his passengers lifted up another.

'Half a dozen like this,' Bill answered, 'and about forty bass. . . Do you want a tow in?'

'Thanks,' I said, starting to wind in my line. 'I'd be grateful.'

No angler, disengaged himself, can regard another winding in with indifference. I was aware that three pairs of eyes were watching my ascending line on which I could detect no additional weight to the sinker and the bait. Up it came. And on the bottom hook was a red gurnard scarcely bigger than the bream that I had put back in the sea at the start of my trip. Oh, that it had been a bass bigger than one of Bill's damned pollack, bigger than any he had ever caught!

I hauled up the anchor, and glad at least that Bill didn't invite me on board his boat, threw him my painter, which he made fast. He put his engine into gear ahead (he'd got a compass of course) and we moved at speed through the fog for home. It was 'plain coffee' all right. But I wasn't going to be beaten. Fog was an infrequent hazard on the Fowey coast. I had a compass on *Amanda,* and I'd have her painted and afloat again in a few days. My first trip would be to the whiting grounds.

6

IT was fortunate that Bill had been able to give me a tow in from near the whiting grounds for the fog lay thick upon the coast all night. Yet it began to clear with the morning sun and the onset of a gentle offshore wind. By lunch time weather conditions seemed in every way perfect. I decided to make another shot, and in spite of Bill's admonition, to do it in the dinghy, for although I had given *Amanda's* hull a first coat of anti-fouling paint, she needed another, and she was still high and dry.

This time I was taking no chances. I packed some food and a thermos of coffee and, of course, *Amanda's* compass. I also bought a couple of mackerel at Percy Varcoe's, the fishmonger's, in case I didn't catch one on my way to the grounds. More confident than ever of success I set off as soon as I had finished my midday meal, and on the ebb tide, was soon approaching the harbour mouth.

Here, almost opposite to where on the Polruan side I had lost that monster unidentified fish, is Readymoney Cove, which with its sandy beach is Fowey's main playground for summer visitors. There are several old cottages built near the water's edge, and in one of them lived happily married friends of ours, the Sullys, George and Jane, with two young children, Jessica and Matt.

George, in his mid forties, had been an infantry officer from the early days of Hitler's war, taking a temporary commission from the O.T.C. of his university. But I had known him a long time before I learned, indirectly, that he had been awarded the Military Cross for conspicuous gallantry in an action against the Japanese in Malaya: that later in the fall of Singapore he had been taken prisoner and endured three and a half years in a Japanese labour camp; that he had held the rank of major on his retirement on general demobilisation.

He was red-haired, with a bristly moustache: powerfully built, showing no physical signs of his years of starvation. He had a placid temperament. He had a slow deliberate way of speaking, almost a drawl. I had never known him angry or irritated, or for that matter in any way excited. He had been my companion on several fishing trips in *Amanda.* When he hooked a fish, and it might be a sizeable one, he simply started to haul in without comment. It would be only a chuckle, if he landed it, but not even a 'damn' if it got off on the way up.

George at present, like so many redundant army officers, was waiting for a civilian job. A skilled handyman, he had been using his leisure reconstructing a small plywood dinghy to take an outboard motor. I sighted him on the beach, the dinghy itself aground, the engine attached. I pulled in.

I had a special interest in that dinghy, for I had found it adrift and filled with water in the harbour one day, and towed it into the beach. It was leaking badly and generally in a state of neglect. I discovered its owner, found that he had used it as a tender to his big moored motor boat and that having acquired a new one, abandoned it as unsafe, as indeed it was. Boats—any sort of boats—to me are living things, and I hate to see them neglected. It was not pretty. Although moulded it was scarcely more than a 'flatty'. But its hull of half-inch 'marine' plywood was sound. If its sides were built up with stouter gunwales, and its frame strengthened it would be a useful craft, and as George had been looking for a dinghy, safe, yet light enough to be used at Readymoney beach I had temporarily plugged its leaks, and towed it along to him.

I hadn't seen it since he had finished the job, and I congratulated him. He had made a virtually new boat of it.

He said, with his usual modesty:

'I'm afraid it's not very professional. There's still a leak along the keel. I've been trying out the engine. A bit of a bind. The connection to the throttle has snapped. I'll have to get it welded. She'll only go at full speed, and upon my soul it nearly lifted the boat out of the water. It's four horse-power by the way.'

Although conceding their utility, I was averse to outboard engines, which since the war have become very much the fashion for pleasure craft, especially for those whose main delight is to travel fast and indulge in the popular sport of water ski-ing. They make an unpleasant noise. They carve up the surface of an otherwise tranquil sea into unnatural waves which set other boats bobbing up and down and can be even dangerous. I was glad anyway that George's concern was to go slow.

It was a powerful-looking engine. Unlike the early types of 'outboards', its upper parts were enclosed in a streamlined metal canopy. It looked absurdly big for a light eight-foot dinghy, but I didn't wish to be discouraging. I told him about my yesterday's adventure, that I was now on my way on a second attempt to reach the whiting grounds. Would he care to join me?

He beamed.

'Splendid! There's nothing I would like better. I'd have to leave a note for Jane. She's in town, shopping. I can anchor my dinghy in case she floats before we get back,' and he added, diffidently, 'What about trying the outboard on your boat? It would save time getting to the grounds. Shall we see if it will fit your transom?'

I would not have dreamt of suggesting this myself, especially in view of his remark that his engine wouldn't go slow. I was always happy at the oars of my dinghy. I had been looking forward to the long pull, the gradually increasing anticipation, trolling all the way even if that meant hooking nothing but gar fish.

I said without enthusiasm:

'We could try, George.'

The transom of a square-sterned boat is the broad planking which forms its after end. The rudder is hinged to this on a sailing boat, or one with an inboard engine. An outboard is simply clamped on to it, and pivots right and left, so that no rudder is needed. He unclamped it, and waded out with it to the stern of my boat, and I was still half wishing that my transom would prove too thick for the jaws of the twin clamps. They did fit however, although with the boat being partly grounded he couldn't start it yet. He was very lightly clad, and as he hurried up the beach to his cottage I yelled after him:

'Bring a sweater with you. It may be cold out at sea and we'll be out a long time!'

He was soon back. We pushed off, and as soon as we were in deep enough water, he pulled the nylon starting cord (another improvement on the rope and pulley of the old-time outboards). The engine opened with a deep roar, and away we went at a prodigious speed, out of the cove, through the harbour mouth for the open sea, with George in the stern seat, steering.

I was on the midship thwart, facing him (and the swiftly receding shore). My feelings were mixed. We were doing at least fifteen knots, three times the cruising speed of *Amanda.* We were ploughing a wake of waves which could have capsized any small craft that had the misfortune to be struck by them broadside on. There was none near our course, however, which with Punch Cross and the red-roofed house in line, George maintained in obedience to my hand signals, for conversation was not easy against the roar of the engine. But he *did* shout, perhaps because he guessed my unspoken thoughts:

'No good trying for a mackerel, eh? Sorry she won't go slower.'

It was indeed no good for trolling. With the heaviest of sinkers the baits would have simply skimmed the surface of the water and even a gar fish could not have matched our speed. In less than five minutes, had we been bound for the Bramblewick whiting grounds, we would have been there. But one thing was pleasantly certain. We were going to reach the Fowey whiting ground all right, and with the weather conditions ideal. I had taken the extra precaution of listening to the one o'clock B.B.C. local forecast. The fine spell was to continue for the next twenty-four hours. There was no mention of mist or fog. Winds would be light and offshore, visibility good on all channel coasts.

True, that although the sun was shining it was not so warm as yesterday. The wind was north but as we were moving with it, it was apparent only as slight ruffling of the surface of the sea. The air was cool but not cold. And swiftly now the details of the coastal view were unfolding: the china-clay 'mountains' beyond St. Austell above the Gribben; Atlantic Bay, and beyond it on the north horizon Bodmin Moor; to the east Pencarrow Head still hiding the watchhouse in the curve of Lantivet Bay. We reached the point where yesterday I had seen the basking sharks, shortly before the fog had enveloped me, and it was less than twenty minutes since we had left Readymoney Cove!

If Bill had been right we were only half a mile short of our destination. The cross and the red-roofed house were in line. My eyes were on Pencarrow Head. And suddenly I saw it—the old watchhouse, just visible beyond the point. I yelled to George:

'Righto. We're there.'

He stopped the engine, and in the silence he said:

'Mission accomplished—eh? And this is where we're going to fish. Splendid! I'm sorry about the engine, Leo. I suppose if I'd been able to make the darned thing go slower we'd have had some mackerel by now. Don't we need them for bait? By Jove, we did whiz along! What about a fag before we start fishing?'

I suspected that he was really proud of his engine's performance, as I would have been myself if it had been *Amanda* which had brought us out so swiftly. Yet he was showing no excitement about the business now in hand. Calmly he lit a cigarette.

I reassured him about the bait. I'd got a few worms left as well as the two bought mackerel. I dropped the anchor, paid out the line. There was a greater depth than where I had anchored in the fog, more evidence that we were on the ground. I filleted one of the mackerel and cut it up into generous pieces. I handed George one of my two handlines so that he could make a start while I was preparing my own rod.

The only real advantage of rod over handline for deep-sea fishing, apart from the convenience of keeping the line neatly wound on to the reel is in its flexibility in dealing with a big fish. It yields like corn in the wind to a sudden pressure instead of presenting complete resistance. With a handline, provided you are wary enough, you let go when you feel such a pressure, letting the line slip through your fingers, hauling in again gently until you feel the fish again.

As with my rod gear, the handlines (and they were very stout) were furnished with fairly heavy sinkers and three-hook paternosters. George, cigarette between his lips, put on the baits and let his line go over.

'What's the drill?' he asked. 'Down to the bottom then raise it up a bit?'

'Yes. I expect there'll be crabs here. Haul in about a yard when you hit the bottom.'

He was still paying out. But my attention was concentrated on my own gear.

'By Jove it's deep,' he said. Then, 'Yes. I'm on the bottom at last. Up a yard did you say?' There was a moment's silence, then, 'Hello. It won't come. Have I fouled the anchor?'

I glanced at the anchor line. We were riding fair from it. George was tugging at his line. Then he said:

'It's coming in a bit. I say—*I think it's a fish.'*

He stood up, spat the unfinished cigarette from his lips and with both hands started to haul. I stood up too, watching his line, but at the same time his face, which bore an expression I had never seen before on a fishing trip, one of real excitement. He was not an expert. He was hauling in too fast. But I felt it was not in my place to offer him advice. The line anyway was a stout one. I got my gaff ready.

'Is it still on?' I said.

He said nothing. The water was crystal clear. I could see his line reaching down for a considerable depth, but its only detectable movement was upwards as he continued to haul, hand over hand as fast as he could go. Then I saw, deep down, a whitish gleam. I couldn't resist shouting:

'Not so fast, George, for God's sake, or you'll lose it.'

He might have been stone deaf. If anything he hauled faster. And now there was not one gleaming white object but three, whirling round and round, but coming nearer. I had the gaff in my hand. Before I could reach the first fish George heaved it on board, a whiting bigger than I had ever seen caught on my Bramblewick grounds, weighing at least four pounds. And in came another, and a third, both just as big, and all three flapping between his legs and entangling themselves in the coils of line.

It might have been through the sheer physical exertion of hauling in his line at such speed, but I was almost sure that George was trembling with excitement. His cheeks were pink, his eyes sparkling.

'Good God! Three of them! It's fantastic! I've never had such a catch. We've struck the grounds all right. Are they whiting? Do you think we're going to catch more? This is splendid. You start fishing, Leo. I'll take these off. I hope we've got plenty of bait. This is just too wonderful.'

No fish displayed on a fishmonger's slab ever looks quite so dead as a dead whiting with its big sad eyes, its gaping mouth, its depressed and almost invisible fins, its unshapely greyish degutted carcass. Mrs. Beeton would not have improved much on this macabre aspect by bending her whiting into rings with the tails thrust into the mouths, no matter how the dish (recommended specially for invalids) was embellished, and ensauced.

But a whiting newly caught, still alive, with its fins erect is a handsome fish. The upper part of its body is brown, finely mottled with purple, and its belly, which gives it its name, has the whiteness and sheen of exquisite porcelain.

I had no box or basket for our fish. They had to be dropped on to the bottom boards. As George refused my help I completed my preparations and let my line go over. My reel was a small one, and even without the check it was a full minute before I touched bottom. Immediately I struck fish. And now my reel proved a bigger handicap, for I could hardly turn it against the sheer weight of what I took to be another three big whiting. My line of synthetic gut was too thin for me to haul by hand.

George had taken off his fish, rebaited, and let his line go over. I was still winding in, when he shouted.

'Got 'em again! My God how they pull! Have you got them too?'

If he had looked at my rod, bent in a semicircle, he need not have asked. At last I sighted the end. There were three fish, the first two the size of his, the one on the bottom hook a small one, which would solve the problem of bait when the mackerel were exhausted. My line was too light for me to risk lifting them. I had to use the gaff, and by the time I had got them in George was dealing with another three, all big.

I stowed my rod as soon as I had unhooked. I took the other handline, and over it went with its three baited hooks. As the sinker touched the bottom I felt the tugs, and breaking the rules started to haul in as fast as I could. Three more big whiting and George, standing up, had his line down again.

This was not angling. Your elderly gentleman, in Harris tweeds, tailored in Savile Row, casting a dry fly for trout with an expensive greenheart rod on the waters of an expensively exclusive chalk stream in the south of England would have been shocked by any suggestion that it was, and even Bill Haley would have sniffed, and said we were no better than the summer trippers who fish with handlines for shad close in to Fowey's lighthouse. But it was terribly exciting, feeling the tugs of those big fish, all the way up from the bottom to the surface and into the boat to join the rapidly growing pile. They were food anyway, and what we could not use ourselves or give to our friends we could sell to Percy Varcoe or the local fried-fish shop.

We went on fishing, oblivious to time, to the fact that our clothes were wet and slimy, that our hands were getting sore with the friction of the lines; oblivious too to the weather, to the fact that we were three and a half miles from the nearest land.

Although the sun still shone from a cloudless sky, the wind had increased. There were little waves where, when we had first dropped anchor, there were only ripples. The boat was dancing at the anchor. We went on fishing, and as well as whiting we were getting whiting pout, and shad weighing up to a pound and more. My own excitement increased when with a big whiting on the top hook came two red gurnard: and it rose to a climax when, with two hooks bare, there was a two-pound John Dory on the third, for apart from its beauty of shape and markings and fantastic dorsal fins, the Dory is even better than gurnard in taste.

Did this beat the Bramblewick grounds of my boyhood? What would the Captain have said if he had seen me haul up that John Dory? Yet there were no flatfish here apparently, no plaice or dabs or sole. But no 'dog' fish either to scare the others away, and put an end to our fishing. I thought loyally that between the two grounds things were standing even. There had been a time when we had caught over two hundred whiting in the *Lydia,* although none bigger than a pound.

At last there came a lull, when neither of us got as much as a nibble. For the first time I realised that I was not only very wet, but very cold. The wind, although no more than a moderate breeze, was north. The sea had become choppy with short steep waves and creaming tops.

I said to George:

'How are you feeling?'

He was still standing up almost knee deep in fish, hands on his line, swaying slightly to the movement of the boat. I noticed that the stern seat was wet and slimy, which may have accounted for his upright posture. He was wearing very thin trousers.

'Fine, Leo, fine,' he answered, not very convincingly. 'Only a bit chilly and I'm dying for a fag, but I don't want to leave go of the line. Anyway my hands are too wet.'

I remembered my thermos flask. I'd stowed it in the bow, the only part of the boat relatively dry and free of fish. I had a spare pullover there too. I knotted my line to a rowlock, and wiping my hands on the pullover was able not only to pour out a beaker full of steaming coffee but also to extract a packet of cigarettes from my pocket and pass one and the coffee to him. But already, looking at the waves, I had realised that the time had come to pack up, and George made no demur when I told him so.

We shared the coffee and a Cornish pasty I had brought. We wound in our lines, which for the first time had no fish on them. I started to haul in the anchor and I had a foretaste of what was to come, for with way on the boat one of those waves broke over the bow drenching me with spray. I got the anchor in. George was bending over the engine, his back towards me. As he pulled at the cord, and nothing happened, I had a moment of alarm. If it wouldn't start, it would be a long and arduous pull home, for there is nothing worse than a choppy sea with short waves for using oars. But the engine did start. Immediately George had to sit down on that wet seat, and steer into sea and wind, the first wave drenching both of us as its spray slapped over the bow.

And that was only the start. The waves were not more than eight feet between crests. Had our speed been less some of them at least could have been taken easily. With a speed-boat hull, the spray would have been thrown aside with its high-raised bow. The dinghy had to slice them.

There was no danger, so long as the wind did not increase, steepening the waves. We were moving towards the lee of the land. Close in along the coast there would be no wind at all. In sheltered Ready-money Cove at this moment children would be paddling and swimming, girls in bikinis sprawling in the sun, even cooling themselves with ice-cream and Coca-Colas. And we had three and a half miles to go.

We were past talking. I was sitting, hatless, on the midship thwart, my back to the spray. I had put on my pullover but through it I could feel the water trickling down my neck and back, and the wind had the venom of an arctic blast. George, also hatless and wearing only a thin sweater over his cotton shirt, was taking the spray full in his face. His hair was drooped over his forehead like the fur of a spaniel emerging from a swim: water was dripping from the end of his nose. He had to keep rubbing it from his eyes, for it must have been half blinding him. His expression was grim, resolute, as it might have been when leading his men into battle.

Yet we were moving, not so fast as on our outward passage with sea and wind in our favour, but certainly at no less a speed than ten knots. Defying the spray I turned to look ahead at intervals. As eagerly as I had looked for the first sight of the watchhouse clearing Pencarrow I shortly saw it disappear behind the point. The 'snow mountains' of St. Austell were slowly sinking behind the cliffs of the Gribben, while the cliffs enlarged.

It was only spray that was coming aboard, no green water. There was no need to bale. It would have been difficult anyway because of the fish which covered all the bottom boards and were slithering about as the boat pitched to the waves. The water itself was not cold. But for that fiendish wind the spray could have been exhilarating, and we could have laughed and enjoyed this climax to a phenomenally successful fishing trip. As it was I was shaking in all my limbs, my teeth chattering, and George, despite his brave expression, could not have been wishing less than I was for the shelter and warmth of the land.

As we drew towards the coast, however, clear of the wide expanse of St. Austell Bay, the waves became appreciably less steep, and with that our speed increased. Ten more minutes and we would be in the lee of the lighthouse cliff, with Readymoney just round the corner, and for the first time George not only smiled but spoke in his more familiar lethargic accents: and again he must have read my thoughts:

'I don't know how you're feeling, Leo, but I'm rather damp, and I think it would be nice to stand under a hot shower, change into dry garments and have a drink of hot toddy, all of which will be available chez nous, for we've got an electric geyser and it shouldn't be our infant's bath time yet. You're not going back to your wifeless home at present, anyway. Besides, you'll need some help to carry the catch to Percy Varcoe's. Is that okay?'

Between chattering teeth I said, 'Okay.'

7

I DON'T remember what year it was, but it was the summer the sharks and the jelly-fish came to Bramblewick Bay and ruined the salmon fishing.

They were blue sharks, from six to eight feet long. Unlike the basking shark they feed on other fish, especially herring. And it was because there were huge shoals of herring fry (they were known as 'sile' and were about the size of a sprat) along the coast that the sharks had appeared. They drove the sile in towards the shore at night time to where in shallow water the salmon fishers shot their nets. The meshes of these nets were big so that the sile swam through them. But the sharks got entangled and lashing with their tails tore the nets to pieces. Some of them were caught, with yards of net and rope wrapped round them, and brought ashore for everyone to see, and that made the people who owned the hotels and summer boarding houses and cafes cross, thinking that the very sight of a shark caught in the Bay would keep away their customers.

The jelly-fish were just as big a pest to the fishermen. They were the big brown ones which the fishermen called 'swarthers'. They were beautiful to look at when you saw them from a boat, with their tentacles waving down from the jelly body like a mass of golden hair. But each of these hairs was made up of tiny poison darts, which stung more fiercely than any nettle, although close up to the body where there was a ring of bigger tentacles, you sometimes could see little fish who used the jelly-fish as a sort of foster mother, and took no harm from the stings.

There were such swarms of jelly-fish that they actually sank some of the salmon nets. Not only were the hands and bare arms of the fishermen stung when they hauled the nets in, when the nets were cleaned and hung out in the sun to dry, the withered tentacles which had clung to the meshes turned to a poison dust which stung the men's eyes like pepper.

One man who had his net damaged so badly that he had to buy a new one was old Neddy Peacock, who was supposed to be the stingiest and most bad-tempered man in the village although he was quite rich, for he was the only coal merchant and he made extra money by selling vegetables from a big garden he owned. He only used his coble for salmon fishing. There had to be two men, one to pull the oars, the other to shoot and haul. His partner was a retired sailor with a lame leg called Tom Skelton. The first time they shot their new net they caught in it, not a shark, but a giant sun-fish. Like some of the sharks it got entangled in the net and the top and bottom ropes, so they had to bring it ashore as it was.

No one had ever seen a sun-fish before, and people, especially the visitors, crowded round when it was hauled up to the Dock. It was the funniest fish that I had ever seen. It was enormous; about seven feet long from mouth to tail and almost as much from its back to its belly yet only about three feet from side to side. It had a tiny mouth that would hardly have swallowed a pennock. Its eyes were small like a pig's. Its side fins were small, too, but it had one big dorsal fin, and one ventral fin just as big, and both of these were joined on to the tail, which didn't look like a real tail but only a part of these two fins.

There were so many people crowding round that Neddy saw that he might make some money out of it. It was dragged up to his coal shed at the far end of the Dock, and he put up a notice on the door to say that anyone who wanted to see the giant sun-fish would have to pay sixpence, with children half price. He and Tom Skelton took turns collecting the money.

In a few days however it began to go bad and stink, and the police sergeant said he would have to move it. So Neddy, who didn't believe in wasting anything, had it carried by his horse and cart up to his garden at the back of the village. He cut it into pieces and buried them to make manure for his winter cabbages and brussels sprouts. But the fishy smell was so strong that it attracted dozens of cats, which killed all his plants by scratching up the soil to get at the bits of fish.

It was a very fine warm summer. Day after day the sea was smooth and there were plenty of fish at the whiting grounds and plenty of mackerel too, chasing the shoals of herring sile. Every day you could see dark patches on the sea far out in the Bay with flocks of gulls and other sea birds wheeling over them. But because of the sharks and the jelly-fish, trade for the pleasure boatmen was very bad.

To make things worse a visitor who was staying at one of the hotels in the village swam into a jelly-fish when he was bathing from the beach. He was stung from head to foot and he was so ill that he had to be taken to hospital. This was reported in the newspapers, which also said that some visitors fishing in the Bay had actually been attacked by sharks, which had tried to capsize the boat. This was a lie and made the village people very angry.

Captain Bunny wasn't afraid of the sharks. Neither was I really, for blue sharks were not man eaters, like some the Captain had seen on his foreign voyages. We did get a few customers for pulling and fishing, but not so many as we would have done if the visitors hadn't been frightened. As Captain Bunny hadn't got much money and depended on the *Lydia* to make him enough to live on through the winter, this made me sad, and when on a Saturday he offered me my penny wage, I told him I didn't want it, but he just laughed and pushed it into my pocket.

One evening of a day late in August when we hadn't had a single customer, although by this time the sharks and jelly-fish had gone, the Captain said as we moored the *Lydia* in the Landing:

'If trade's no better than this tomorrow we ought to see if we can't make a bit of brass fishing. Start off in the morn taking a bit o' grub with us, and make a day of it. There's no one else bringing in much fish at present. A good catch of plaice and dabs and mackerel would pay better than visitors giving us a bob an hour and them taking the fish too. We could use the sails. Better than pulling, especially for mackerel. If it was plain coffee on the whiting grounds, and there was a nice breeze we could sail up southwards and try Stoupe Beck grounds, where there's sometimes some nice plaice. There's not likely to be any visitors wanting a boat tomorrow, for it's Whitby Regatta.' And then he said, 'But maybe you'll want to go there yourself, eh?'

I felt awful. I *was* going to the regatta. In spite of my liking to be with the Captain and *Lydia* so much, I had been looking forward to it all summer for I had never been before. I had been told by the other lads that it was very exciting. Apart from yacht and boat racing there was a greasy pole, a thick mast covered with soft soap, sticking out from a pier over the water with a leg of mutton at the end of it as a prize.

There was a fair, with swings and roundabouts and coconut shies. There was even a competition for pennock fishing for lads under fourteen years of age, and I thought there might be a chance of my winning.

Although we were very poor and there would be the train fare to pay, Mother had said I could go. I had been saving up my wages and tips. If I told the Captain now that I wouldn't be able to go with him tomorrow it might mean that he would lose the chance of making some money, or that he might ask some other lad to go with him. Besides, although we had sometimes gone fishing by ourselves when there were no customers, we'd never done it for a whole day, and we had never used the *Lydia's* sails. I thought that if I did go to the regatta I would be thinking all the time about how the Captain was getting on, and if he was catching more fish than he had ever caught before. And just the same if I went with him, I would be thinking of what I was missing, especially if we didn't catch a lot of fish. But he had been so kind, and I liked him so much that I couldn't even tell him that I wanted to go to the regatta. I just said that I would like to go with him and didn't mention the regatta at all. And all he said when we parted at the slipway top was:

'All right then. Nine o' clock. Have a good breakfast, and ask your mother to pack up some grub, and tell her we won't be back till tea time. But it's got to be good weather, think on—it's got to be good weather.'

It was good weather. It was a perfect day. The wind was west, but not too strong. The sun was hot with little round clouds in the sky, that never really covered it. It was perfect weather for the regatta too, but I wasn't thinking about the regatta when just after nine o' clock we cast off from our mooring, and with the wind filling our sails (mainsail and jib) we speeded out of the Landing for the whiting grounds.

As we cleared the posts which mark the Landing mouth the Captain said:

'Out with the spinner. We're clear of the tangles, and unless we're going over fast this is a likely spot for a billet or a sprag.'

I put the line over, but we must have been going too fast, for I caught nothing and within a few minutes the Captain told me to wind in, for we had reached, the grounds. Down came the sails, over went the anchor, and we started to fish. The last time we'd been to the whiting grounds about a week before, with some day visitors who hadn't heard about the sharks, the whiting had started biting straight away, and we'd got a nice lot of flatfish too, all of which the visitors had taken. Now we waited a long time before the Captain got the first bite and when he hauled in it was only a little dab. After a while he said:

'Why—this looks like plain coffee. All the fish must have gone off to the regatta. Do you think we'd best give it up and gan home?'

I knew he was only joking, but it did make me think about the regatta and wish a bit that I'd gone, if only to try and win the prize for the pennock competition. But all the time the Captain's eyes had been roving seawards and suddenly he shouted and pointed:

'Eh—look over yonder. Aren't them gulls on

t' watter? They're after sile, and where there's sile there'll be mackerel. Wind your line in. I'll soon have the anchor up, and the sails set. That'll be better sport than this.'

I started to wind in my line, but at once I felt a good tug. I shouted:

'I've got one. A good one, too. Don't let's go yet. He's a good one.'

'Steady then—don't lose him.'

I hauled in steadily, feeling the fish tugging all the time, and then I swung it on board, a lovely plaice with bright red spots on its pale-green back. I had never known the Captain so pleased with a fish. Perhaps, I thought, it was because he'd be able to sell it, instead of putting it on a string for a visitor to take free. It would be worth at least half an ounce of 'baccy'. He kept on saying:

'It's a beauty—it's a beauty!'

I said:

'Don't you think we ought to stay here, now we've started?'

'Nay. Not when there's mackerel about and there's a wind for sailing. We can always come back. Wind will very likely drop later on. Look at them gulls now. There's swarms of them. Get the trolling line over as soon as I get the anchor up and the sails set.'

The gulls were about a mile seawards and towards the south end of the Bay. We were soon near enough to see what they were. Most of them were herring gulls, but there were a number of black backers, and kittiwakes and black heads, and a few snow-white gannets which were dropping down into the sea, going under and then soaring up with their beaks full of sile. There were ordinary cormorants too, and guillemots and puffins (which had beaks like parrots) and razor-bills, but these were just singly, some distance from the screaming gulls. We saw a razor-bill come up from a dive with a small mackerel in its beak. It got such a fright coming up so near to the boat that it dropped the mackerel and dived again. A big black-backed gull swooped down and snapped it.

It was just then I got my first bite. I hauled in. It was a full-size mackerel, not like the one the razor-bill had caught and lost. We couldn't use two trolling lines at the same time or they would get entangled by the fish, and I said to the Captain:

'It's your turn now.'

He laughed.

'Nay. You keep at it. We're going straight through the shoal now. Can't you smell 'em? There's sile all round us. See that broken watter ahead. There's mackerel driving the sile up.'

I was too excited to look at anything properly. The gulls were wheeling all round us making a terrific din. Perhaps they thought we were trying to rob them of their prey. I certainly could smell fish, and I saw some sile breaking the water just like a shower of hailstones, and with the splash of bigger fish among them, but as soon as the spinner was overboard there was another mackerel on it, and the same thing happened as soon as it was over again.

It went on like this until there were at least a dozen fine mackerel in the fishbox. All the time I had been fishing while the Captain just steered, sailing backwards and forwards round the shoal, which meant, of course, that every few minutes he would have to change tacks, hauling in the sheet and tacks of the sails from one side to the other. I had never sailed a boat, of course, but I was learning how it was done. I kept on begging him to let me try so that he could fish, and at last, just as we had changed tacks and with the wind not blowing so strong, he let me take the tiller. The line was overboard. He took it. I was praying that he would get a fish straight away, and go on catching them as I had been doing.

But he didn't. We were about a hundred yards away from the gulls when I had taken the tiller. I steered towards them, but the sails had started to flap, and the *Lydia* went slower and slower, and instead of moving towards the shoal she turned of her own accord, and almost stopped. The sea, which had been quite choppy, started to become smooth and shiny except here and there where there were still puffs of wind. And another thing had happened. The gulls had stopped screaming and wheeling round and round. They were just floating on the sea. There was no sign of breaking fish. The sile and the mackerel too, must have gone down to deep water.

The Captain didn't seem a bit disappointed. The trolling line, with its heavy sinker was falling straight down, and he hauled it in for half its length, in case the spinner fouled the bottom.

'I wish you could catch one,' I said. 'You go on fishing while I pull with the oars.'

He laughed.

'Nay. That'll be no good for mackerel. We'll not go fast enough, unless both of us pull our hardest and it's going to be ower hot for that. We'll pull in for Stoupe Beck Sands. We're more than halfway there already. We'll have a try for a plaice and dabs, and when we anchor we'll have a bit of summat to eat and a pipe of baccy. But we'll keep the spinner over while we pull. We might get a codling or a billet. I'll put a strip of mackerel on the spinner. Cod like to take a smell at a bait before they swallow it.'

I had scarcely noticed until now how far to the south of the Bay we had sailed. We were not more than a mile from the big cliff which makes the south end of the bay, and less than that was a stretch of sandy beach where a little stream called Stoupe Beck, came down from the moors to the sea.

We stowed the sails and started pulling straight in towards the shore. The Captain pulled the after oars, but he held the line within the grasp of his right hand, which gave it an extra jerking movement. Nothing happened for quite a time, and I wasn't looking at him when he gave a shout, let go of his oars, and started to haul in.

'Have you got one?' I yelled.

'Aye. If he doesn't get off. A good 'un too. Must be a codling. Here he comes!'

There was a splash, and he swung his first catch into the boat. It was a big gurnard. As he took it off the hook a number of sile fell from its mouth. Everything was just perfect I felt, now that the Captain had broken his luck. He didn't catch another, however. We went on pulling, but every now and then he turned to look ahead to where near the edge of the cliff there was a farm-house, and I guessed he was looking for the bearing marks of the fishing ground. Shortly he said:

'This is about it. Stoupe Beck Sand reaches for nearly a mile seawards with patches of rock here and there. If it wasn't such a long way from the Landing more pleasure boats would come here to fish. It's as good a ground as t' other one. Ship your oars, and heave the anchor over.'

He wound in the trolling line. We re-baited the chopsticks, but as soon as his was down the Captain made his fast, and wiped the sweat from his brow with a big red handkerchief.

'It must be nigh dinner time,' he said. 'What about having a bite to eat and summat to drink, and then for me a pipe of baccy while we're waiting for them to start biting?'

Before I could answer I felt a tug.

'Have you got one?'

'Think so,' I said, hauling in.

The Captain seized his line.

'Why, I have. Aye, I've got one. Two by the feel of it.'

'So have I!' I yelled as I pulled two whiting on board.

'A whiting and a nice dab.' The Captain joined in, holding up his catch. 'We needn't think about dinner yet.'

'No fear, Captain! There must be swarms of fish about.'

The next fish I caught was a gurnard, as big as the Captain's. It pulled stronger than two whitings. But the Captain's next was two plaice, not so big as the one I had caught first but a good size, and it wasn't long before I got another. We soon lost count of what we were catching. There were haddock as well as whiting. There were dabs as well as plaice, and gurnard, and also one small codling, and this must have gone on for nearly an hour before the fish stopped biting. I was really glad because I was aching with hunger.

And yet I don't think I would have enjoyed our meal if the Captain hadn't firmly decided that we must haul up our lines, for as he said, they might come back any moment. Even when we finished our meal he said that he was going to wait a bit longer as he wanted to have a pipe and he couldn't cut and roll his baccy proper if his hands were wet and slimy with fish, but there was no harm in my starting.

The fish had come back, and although the Captain had lit his pipe he couldn't resist starting. He couldn't stop to re-light it when it went out, although he kept it in his mouth, and once or twice nearly lost it overboard in his excitement. At last they stopped again. The Captain made his line fast, re-lit his pipe and I began to fear that our day's sport was over. My heart sank when he said:

'Plain coffee, eh? Things are getting quiet and no mistake. Maybe we've caught them all.' But his eyes were twinkling. To my joy he went on: 'Maybe there'll be some billet closer in. Shall we have a try? I'll take the spinner off the trolling line and put on a couple of billet flies and a lighter lead.'

A billet fly is simply a white feather tied to a bare hook. As soon as he had rigged the line we hauled the anchor and pulled in closer to the shore, keeping on the scaur side of the sand. The tide was nearly up now. The water was so still and clear that soon we could see the bottom. We were just about where the tide would ebb at low spring. There were beds of tangles and patches of shingle. Quite clearly I saw purple sea urchins clinging to the tangles.

Then, as the Captain pulled nearer into the shore, we saw an extraordinary sight.

There was a shoal of fish, all about the same size and about a foot long, packed close together, not moving and all facing the same way. They were lying close to the bottom in what at low tide would be a creek between two scaurs. There were so many of them we couldn't see the actual bottom.

They were billet, grown-up 'pennocks' but only half-grown-up coal fish, which the fishermen sometimes caught on their long lines. The Captain pulled so that we moved between the sunken scaurs and over the shoal and he must have gone fifty yards before he came to the end of it. He had told me to keep on jerking the flies so that they would look like live sile. We passed straight through the shoal. I didn't get a single bite. He turned and pulled back again. The fish hadn't moved, although the flies must have touched some of them. They might have been asleep. Again I began to fear that the Captain would decide to pack up for home. Again my anxiety was relieved, for when we had pulled over the shoal once more he said:

'Why now, it's no use at present. Them fish is waiting for the sile to come in. They're thinking of sile and nowt else, and the sun's too bright and t' watter over clear for them to mistake a feather for one. What we've got to do is wait too. We can't gan home when there's fish about as thick as this. We'll pull ashore and give our legs a stretch. We might find a bit of kindling and light a fire and hot up our tea. Haul in your line.'

He pulled ashore. We got out and carried the anchor up the shingly beach. There was plenty of drift-wood, dried by the sun at high-water mark. We made a fire and put the Captain's billy-can on it. He split two of the mackerel, made a toasting fork out of a stick, and grilled them over the glowing embers. They were delicious. When we had eaten them he sat on a boulder puffing at his pipe but all the time looking out to sea, and I knew he was thinking of that great shoal of billet, lying in wait for the sile.

They were not the only ones waiting. Farther on along towards the south cliff the beach was white with gulls, and suddenly we saw them fly up, screaming as though a gun had gone off. At the same time a patch of water farther out than where we had seen the billet went dark. The gulls flew over it. The sile were in.

The billet were after them too. We could see them breaking water as we pulled towards that patch. As soon as we were near, the Captain made me ship my oars and put the line over. At once it was seized by a fish. It was a billet. It didn't pull as hard as a mackerel, although it was bigger. The next time I got two, and the Captain agreed to let me pull while he fished. By this time we were in the middle of a shoal of sile. They were jumping out of the water as the billet chased them, and each time the oars dipped among them. There must have been millions of them. They looked as though they were made of silver. The wonder was that the billet should go for our feathers when all they had to do was swim along with their mouths open and swallow the real sile. They must have gone mad.

And I think we'd gone a bit mad too with excitement as in turns we hauled the fish in. The Captain had forgotten about his pipe. And billet were not the only fish. There were mackerel, too, and gurnard and even codling, all biting at the feathers. And, of course, if this had happened a few weeks ago there would have been sharks. I wasn't sorry that they'd all gone, although I would like to have seen a live sun-fish.

And what was pleasing me as much as catching the fish was that even if the Captain got only a penny each for them he would make more money than if we'd had visitors with us every day of the week.

The sun was getting low when at last, although the fish were still biting, he said we must give up and make for home. By an extra bit of luck the wind had risen again not very strong, but still west and enough for us to hoist the sails and keep the trolling line over for anything we might catch on our way.

It was the end of the happiest of all my days with Captain Bunny, with no regrets that I had missed the regatta and the chance of winning the pennock-catching prize. It was also nearly my last. Just before next Whitsuntide, when the *Lydia* was due to be re-painted and then launched down from her winter berth, he had a stroke from which he never recovered.

Dear old Captain, with his rosy, Father Christmas cheeks and twinkling eyes, and ever-ready smile! For him there must be a Happy Fishing Ground.

8

CATCHING fish with a net is not angling in the noblest meaning of the word, but it can be very exciting, and provides those elements of suspense and anticipation without which any sort of fishing would be dull.

For net fishing a boat is essential. At 'Bramblewick' it was only done professionally by the summer salmon fishers, for the local fishery by-laws prohibited the use of any sort of net in shallow waters except under licence, and with strict conditions regarding length and depth of net, size of mesh and, more important still, season, which lasted six months, with no fishing allowed on Sundays.

Similar conditions apply to the salmon and salmon trout net fishing in the Fowey River estuary, and its creeks, with the exception that a net of any size mesh can be used for the capture of sand eels (the most popular bait for the bass fishers) and for mullet, provided that such nets are not left unattended, and that if salmon or salmon trout are caught in them they will be released.

The number of net fishers granted licences for salmon is restricted. Fishing is only carried out in daylight, and at small shallow sections of the estuary at certain states of the tide. The net is shot out from the bank from a boat, its end anchored, with a long line brought back from the anchor to the shore, the net, bellying with the current into the shape of a letter D, forming a trap for any fish swimming with the current, a trap which is closed when the anchor line is hauled ashore. The licence is £10 a year, the net expensive. Two men are required to handle net and boat, and while it is an interesting operation to watch, especially when the last section of net comes ashore and you see a mighty salmon kicking in it—a salmon that would go a long way to defraying the cost of the licence—I was never envious. The laws controlling the taking of salmon are wise. Without them the King of Fish long ago would have become extinct in British waters.

The mullet were a different proposition. Living as we did practically on the shore of one of the estuary tidal creeks, and with a little cove of our own, these fish had offered to me a frequent provocation and challenge. They were grey mullet, a species which with local variations is found in many parts of the world, but very rarely on my native Yorkshire coast where an odd one is occasionally caught in the salmon nets.

Like bass, they have silvery scales and belly with blue-grey backs. They are armoured with big tough scales. Their flesh is delicious. They range in size up to twelve pounds. They are gregarious and are found in shoals, which like mackerel sometimes break up into individual groups, or even feed singly. They have very small, practically toothless mouths and their principal food, like the toothless whales and basking sharks is plankton and algae.

Their movements, their comings and goings are unpredictable.

At any time of the year, but usually in spring and in calm weather, I might look out of my study window, which faced the cove and creek, and at half-flood tide see a dark patch, like a shadow in the main channel of the creek, moving only with the flowing tide. I would pull out in the dinghy and try trolling at the edge of the shoal with light tackle and worm for bait. If the light was right I could actually see the fish, packed in an almost solid mass, heads up-stream, their bellies flashing here and there, the only sign that some of them were self-propelled and not just drifting. On no occasion did I succeed in persuading one of the multitude to take interest in my bait.

The creek ended in a cul-de-sac, where a stream entered it. There was also a little stream flowing into our own cove. It was obvious that it was the mixture of salt water with fresh, and the food it contained, that attracted the fish in from the open sea. Unfortunately there was a small village and boat houses at the creek end and when the water was deep enough there would often be a motor boat passing up or down which would have the effect of scattering the shoal, or driving them to the bottom. Sometimes, however, I would not see a shoal at all, but at high water the fish would be scattered over the whole creek. And quite regularly throughout spring and summer there would be several mullet which swam leisurely into our own cove when the tide was high enough, so close in that their dorsal fins were breaking the surface.

At the slightest sound of footsteps they would swim out again. I had tried stalking them, moving to the water's edge on my hands and knees, then flicking the bait on top of them. I had tried approaching them from the side of the cove with my landing net, then making a sudden rush, half throwing the net at them. They would elude it, swim out, yet in ten minutes if I kept dead still they would be back in shallow water, to mock me.

Curiously enough, it was with the landing net

that I caught my first mullet, and I am convinced that it was because it was asleep. I was in the dinghy just clear of the cove. It was a warm day, the water calm and clear. I saw it, not more than two feet from the surface, not moving except for a slight vibration of its pectoral fins, proof at least that it was alive. Without the slightest hope of success, I dipped the net in slowly until it was close to and slightly below the fish. It did not move. I swooped and jerked the net up and over the gunwale, the fish falling out on to the bottom board, where it lay, kicking madly as though indeed it had been awakened from a peaceful sleep. It was a beauty, too, weighing over three pounds. And I was almost sorry to dispatch it, it was like hitting a man when he was down.

I bought a net in the end. It was second-hand, sixty yards in length, two fathoms deep with one-and-a-half-inch mesh, corks on the head rope, weighted with lead pellets on the foot.

It was what is known as a mesh net, like those used for herring, pilchard and mackerel. The fish encountering it try to push their pointed snouts through a mesh. The thin cord slides easily over their gill covers but no farther because of the thickness of the body. When the fish tries to wriggle back the gill covers, which are 'hinged' at the fore end, rise. The fish are trapped.

But few fish are foolish enough to swim into a net in broad daylight, with the water clear. The Fowey salmon were not meshed. Because of the swift current the estuary water flowing over a muddy bottom was never clear. They were caught in that D-shaped bag, to escape from which they would have to reverse their up-stream or down-stream movement and swim along the wall of net until they came to the moored end, which probably a certain number of them would do.

To catch mullet I would obviously have to use my net at night, and the later and darker the better. It would be best to do it soon after high water when the tide was ebbing and the mullet, if there were any in the upper reaches of the creek, were on their way back to the deep water of the harbour or to the sea. I had observed that those which impudently haunted the cove by day never appeared in similar conditions of tide at night. It was a reasonable guess that they moved higher up the creek on the flood and that as they had such a liking for the cove they might at least swim near to it on the ebb. It would be rough justice if they were my first victims.

Amanda was moored about forty yards outwards from the mouth of the cove, which had low cliffs on each side. My plan was to fix one end of the net to the cliff nearer to harbour where at high tide there was a depth of six feet, and shoot it out to *Amanda* where I would make fast its other end. The tide should belly it in the direction of the harbour. Any fish swimming with the tide, unless meshed would like the salmon, have to follow the net out to *Amanda* to get clear.

I had to wait several days for what seemed to be the right conditions of light, or rather darkness, weather and state of tide. It was early summer before the holiday season had really started. The day had been fine and warm and we had been bathing in the cove. Possibly this had kept my tormenting fish from paying their usual close-in visitation. But a small shoal had gone up the creek on the morning flood. By tea time a change had come in the weather. Although there was no wind, the sky became overcast and misty and a drizzle began to fall which changed to light rain later in the evening, advancing the coming of dark.

High water however was not until eleven. By then my family were in bed and asleep, and I moved down quietly, almost surreptitiously from the house to the cove, a distance of not more than fifty yards. Familiar though I was with the path it was so dark I had to use my torch.

It was still raining gently, a warm noiseless summer rain. I halted at the water's edge, where the dinghy was just afloat, the net stowed ready on the stern seat. I switched off my torch and stood for a while with my ears strained. Even in fog there is never absolute dark at night in the open air. Vaguely I could distinguish the opposite hilly bank of the creek, and the shape of *Amanda.* Through the dead quiet I could hear faintly, and yet not far from the shore a plopping sound, a sound which could only have been made by rising fish, for there was no wind, the water now at the slack of high tide was motionless.

I got into the dinghy, and with a single oar sculled to the point where I was to secure the shore end of the net. I had, during daylight, fixed a stout rope to a branch of a tree overhanging the cliff. I picked up its end, tied the headline to it and pushed off, sculling with one hand, paying out the net with the other, steering for *Amanda.* With the tide still slack it paid out straight, and although it snagged on the gunwale once or twice and I had to stop to clear it, I was soon within reach of *Amanda's* stern, and I was able to grip it with one hand, holding the net with the other, and hauling it in until there was enough slack to make it fast. I switched on my torch then, and directed its beam along the line of corks leading back to the shore. The net was well and truly laid, and I had done it just in time, for already

Amanda was swinging head up creek, the net began to curve towards the harbour.

How long should I give it before I hauled? The tides were halfway between neap and spring. I must haul before the shore end grounded. That would be, I reckoned, in about an hour. During that time, if I was to obey the law I must not leave it unattended. I made the dinghy fast, got into *Amanda,* and lit a cigarette.

An hour was a long time to wait. Should I, say in half an hour, without hauling, move along the net at the bellied side in the dinghy, and with the torch see if there were any fish in it? I could still hear those plopping sounds and some of them on the shore side of *Amanda,* not far from the net itself. It might be that the shoal I had seen that morning was already swimming straight towards it. But I should know, by a more definite splashing, if any of them had struck. I must be patient. I lit another cigarette from the stub of the first.

Shortly however I did hear a splash. I switched on the torch, shone it along the net and in its beam I saw a fish—it must have been a mullet—sail like a flying fish over the corks and fall with a splash on the other side, and within a second, another follow it. Were they my tormentors, or did they belong to the shoal? If they belonged to the shoal, were they all going to behave like this and escape? I had already imagined the net full of mullet, enough to half-fill the dinghy. Perhaps some of them, not as agile, were already meshed. But if I turned on the torch again that possibly would make it visible to the fish which were hesitating, and turn them back. I must wait, even though the suspense was becoming almost unbearable, and I lit another cigarette. I must have smoked half a packet when, with a quarter of that hour still to go, I could stand it no longer.

I got into the dinghy, hauled in the heavy sinker I had fixed on this end of the foot rope, untied the headline from *Amanda* and, keeping both lines together with the net doubled between so as to form a 'bag', started to haul in over the dinghy's stern. Again I heard the splash of fish as they leapt over the net only a few feet ahead of me. But there was nothing in the net itself except seaweed, a bottle, a cardboard carton and other rubbish which had floated down on the tide, not a single fish. I was hauling quickly too. Very soon I would reach the end tied to the cliff where I judged there was still enough water to float the dinghy.

By now I had lost all' hope. And then with not more than ten feet of the net to come in, I heard another splash. I felt a jerking on the net itself. I switched on my torch and saw close into the cliff among the floating weed something gleaming white. I continued to haul, still not certain that what I had seen was in the net: the net itself was now twisted and wrapped round both ropes. The weight of it increased as though it had become entangled on the bottom. I gave a final heave, and the next moment it came on board, a muddle of net and rope; in that muddle an object which, by the way it was struggling, I knew to be not only a fish, but a big one.

I could not see it. It had fallen on the bottom boards, and in my excitement I had knocked over the whole pile of net on top of it, my torch too. I could hear it flapping however, as I groped for my torch among the net and the seaweed and other rubbish I had hauled in. I struck a match. It gave me enough light to spot the torch, which I had to hold in one hand while I cleared the net with the other, and at last got a sight of the fish itself, still wrapped up in net, still flapping madly to get free. It was not, as I had imagined and hoped, a mullet. *It was a salmon trout,* weighing at a guess, round about five pounds.

From the moment of identification I was tempted of the devil. A salmon or salmon trout caught otherwise than by a licensed fisherman and other proscribed legal regulations had to be returned alive to the river or sea. This one was still very much alive. It wasn't meshed. It was much too big for that. It had struck the net and got wrapped in it in rage and frustration.

It was as though two voices were speaking to me, that of the devil, with whom I had a longstanding acquaintance, the other of my conscience. The devil was saying 'What a splendid fish, making up for all the mullet that have escaped. How excited your wife and little girl will be to see it in the morning. What a dish for them to eat. Don't worry about the law. Who's going to find out anyway, at this time of night? Take it home.' And the voice of conscience saying and not quite so convincingly, 'Let it go, let it go. The law was made to prevent the extinction of the salmon. You must let it go.'

Obliged to hold the torch in one hand, I realised the futility of trying to disentangle it from the net with the other. I used my knife, ruthlessly cutting through the meshes near its head. I gripped and pulled it loose, then, dropping the torch, I picked the fish up with both hands. And neither the devil nor my conscience won the battle. For it gave a sudden mighty kick, slipped from my hands and went overboard into the creek.

9

NATURALLY I was interested in seeing how Fowey's experts set about catching mullet. One of these was my old friend Percy Varcoe, the fishmonger and one-time Mayor of Fowey, who, with his assistant shopkeeper and 'partner' Tony, fished for salmon in the season and for mullet whenever the opportunity came.

Percy had been a professional footballer as a young man and for many seasons had played in the forward line for Aston Villa. But fishing was in his blood, as much for the fun of it as for profit, and he preferred it, I was sure, to serving customers in his shop. He was heavily built, clean shaven, with an open generous face, a jolly disposition and walked with a sailor's roll. He had a strong Cornish accent, and as in non-business hours he usually spoke with a cigarette in his mouth I had difficulty in understanding what he said. But at a social, to which we were invited, he made a brilliantly witty extempore speech, and had the whole assembly in fits of laughter.

Tony was a naturalised Pole, born in Gdynia. Of fisherman stock, he had served in the Polish Navy during the late war, and chance had brought him to Fowey, then a base for assault craft. He had fallen in love with a local girl, married her and settled in Fowey after the war. Like most Poles and especially sailors, he was good-looking. He had learned to speak English, but it was with a Cornish accent and, when he got excited, with a mixture of words from his native tongue. Again I had difficulty in following what he said. It was clear he and Percy understood each other perfectly.

They had two boats, a stout twenty footer with a powerful marine engine, and a fourteen-foot pulling boat used for netting. I had evidence that they knew how to catch mullet. On several occasions I had seen them land at the Albert Quay, with the pulling boat laden down with fish. There were several other tidal creeks besides our own branching from the main estuary where the shoals were found. One of their biggest hauls had been in Readymoney Cove. But I had never seen them in action.

It was an afternoon in late October, mild and misty, with the creek calm when I heard the tug-tug of Percy's big boat engine and shortly saw him and Tony, with the rowing boat in tow, moving slowly up the creek close in to our side of it, disappearing behind the rocky point of the cove. Taking my field-glasses, I climbed up the hill above the house from which I had a clear view of the whole creek. I saw that they had anchored about a hundred yards up from the cove. They were standing up on the thwarts of the big boat, looking intently towards the opposite shore. In the middle of the creek was a dark purplish patch, unmistakably a shoal of mullet, and an unusually big one too. It was the slack of a neap tide, with no apparent current. The shoal seemed to be static, as I had so often seen when I had pulled round one with my trolling line, the fish packed close together almost touching each other, and in layers too, reaching down from the surface.

With my glasses, which were powerful ones I used for bird watching, I could see the net piled up in the stern of the pulling boat, obviously many times bigger than my own. I guessed that it would be of similar size of mesh, but that they would use it in the same way as they did their salmon net, only without an anchor, operating from the shore, shooting straight out and then in a curve that would surround the shoal, then back to the shore. If they did that quickly some of the fish would undoubtedly jump over the net and escape, but the majority would be trapped and hauled ashore.

The shoal, however, was almost in the middle of the creek, although slightly nearer to the opposite shore. It would take an immensely long net to reach out there to it and back. They would have to wait for the tide in the hope that the fish would move with it on a course nearer to one of the shores. I was tempted to go down and pull along in the dinghy for a closer view. But by doing so, I might disturb the shoal and upset Percy's plan. I decided to stay where I was, watching with my glasses both fishers and the fish themselves.

Percy as usual had a cigarette between his lips. But apart from spitting the stub out and lighting another, neither he nor Tony moved or relaxed their watch. At least a quarter of an hour elapsed before the shoal started to move very slowly down-creek proving only that the tide had turned. It was still slightly nearer to the opposite bank, still out of range of the net.

I was resting my eyes from the strain of the glasses when I heard the distant sound of a motor, up-creek. A boat was moving down it. Percy must have heard it too. He was looking up-creek, and had raised his hand, as a warning signal. Tony did the same as the boat, it was a dinghy with an outboard, approached, and I heard Percy shout as he pointed towards the shoal, warning the occupant of the boat to steer in for it was moving down the middle of the creek.

The warning must have been misunderstood. The occupant of the dinghy, a youth from one of the farms at the head of the creek, evidently thought that Percy was warning him away from his own boats. He steered outwards instead of in, straight for the shoal and had almost reached it when frantic shouts caused him to swing away, and carry on down-creek. When I looked again, there was no sign of the shoal. Percy was hauling in the anchor.

But Tony was still on watch. As the anchor came on board I saw him point to the opposite shore where there was a shallow indentation and a narrow shingle beach. Percy had swung round and was staring in that direction, and again I saw the purple patch, not so big as it had been before, but certainly mullet not more than ten yards out from the beach.

Percy had dropped the anchor again. They pulled the small boat alongside, got in, and Tony began to scull down-creek from the beach. I was so excited now I could not hold the glasses steady, but with my naked eyes I saw that the patch was growing bigger as more of the fish surfaced. It must be the same shoal that the dinghy had scared. The boat grounded. Percy got out. The boat was turned so that its bow was pointing outwards. The end of the net was made fast ashore. The inner edge of the shoal was still close into the beach. Tony stood ready with the sculling oar. Percy gave the stern of the boat a gentle push, and away it went, Tony sculling with one hand, paying out the net with the other.

He hadn't gone four lengths when I heard the sound of a motor which at first I took to be that of a plane. It got nearer, louder. Coming up the creek from the harbour was a speed-boat throwing two plumes of spray from its bows. Tony stopped shooting, held up a warning hand. It was no good. There was a young man and a girl in the boat, the girl's hair streaming in the wind like the advertisements for speed-boats which you see in American glossy magazines. Even if they had seen Tony's signals, and probably they didn't, they were going so fast, it would have been no good. They shot past within a few yards of him, their bow wave throwing the boat almost on its beam ends; Tony had to hang on to the pile of net to stop it going overboard. The wave rolled ashore, breaking on the beach. Halfway up the creek the speed-boat turned, banking like an aeroplane and came back, producing another wave against the back-wash from the shore, shot past again, the girl in all innocence actually waving her hand to Tony and Percy. Perhaps she mistook their answering wave as a token of admiration, not noticing that Tony's fists were clenched. The shoal of course had gone.

*

It was not until shortly after the onslaught of the dramatic winter of 1962-3 that I saw Percy and Tony in action with the mullet again. It was in the early weeks of January. Although most of England had already become snow-bound, there had been only a slight fall in the Fowey coastal area. But there was a severe and relentless frost, so severe that although the harbour and estuary did not freeze, blocks of ice like miniature icebergs floated down from the upper reaches of the river. And on the beaches were scores of dead fish, mostly wrasse, but including many big congers, the congers with their eyes glazed, supporting a widely held theory among fishermen, Yorkshire as well as Cornish, that the cold blinds them, so that they swim ashore by mistake, a theory disputed by the academic sea biologists.

Close to Fowey railway station is a tidal creek called Caffa Mill Pill, a refuge for boats in bad weather. A fresh-water stream runs into it, and at high tide it is a favourite spot for mullet, usually small ones, the size of our 'Bramblewick' pennocks. I had gone to the station that day to collect a parcel. I was just in time to see my friends shooting their net across the Pill, from the quay side to the railway embankment, completely shutting it off from the deep water of the harbour. Shoreward of it, trapped but still too close in to the head of the Pill to be aware of it, was a shoal of mullet, almost as big as the one on that earlier unlucky occasion.

From the quay wall I had a perfect view of them. There must have been several hundreds, most of them about a pound in weight, all with their heads pointing to where the stream entered at the embankment foot. The tide was ebbing. There was a narrow beach at the head of the Pill. Long ropes from each end of the net led into this beach, but they were still slack.

It was bitterly cold. There was a thin layer of ice on the salt water of the Pill. But Percy and Tony were wearing only jerseys with sleeves rolled up and, of course, rubber thigh-boots. They had moved to the beach, leaving their boat at the quay, outside the net which was to prove a wise precaution. Thinking that I might be of some assistance I climbed down to the beach too. There were a few other spectators, all male. I said to Percy (again with a cigarette in his mouth):

'You've got them this time!'

'Don't know about that,' he answered. 'We won't know till we've got 'em ashore. Ground hereabouts is rough. '

He had started to haul in the slack of one of the ropes, but he waved me aside when I moved to help. He was doing it gingerly, keeping the corks near to the enclosing wall. Tony was on the other rope doing the same. Then with all the slack in they began to haul faster, the net drawing on to the fish. The alarm had been sounded. A big mullet leapt clear of the corks and several more followed in quick succession. Inside the net it was as though the water was boiling as the fish were pressed in. Both men were straining at the ropes now. And Percy gave a sudden shout:

'We've fouled something, Tony. Stop hauling.' And to me, 'Take his end, hang on, don't haul.'

I took the rope. Tony rushed along the quay to the boat, pushed off and sculled along the outside of the net to a point where some of the corks had gone under water, leaving a gap through which more fish were escaping, one of them actually jumping into the boat itself. With a boat-hook he reached down to clear the bottom of the net from the obstacle it had fouled. He soon gave up, and bending low over the gunwale, he tried with his hands, reaching down to his shoulders into the freezing water. He was tugging at something, and shortly he started to heave, and up came an old rusty anchor, round the flukes of which the net was fast. He cleared it. The corks floated again, and Percy shouted to me to start hauling, not waiting for Tony. But Tony was soon back and we were pulling together. The net was grounding, odd fish still escaping. But the bulk of the shoal was in the bag – hundreds and hundreds of them, not one under a pound in weight, many of them much bigger, some of them meshed, but the majority of them just to be picked up and thrown into the baskets ready on the beach.

It was going to be a long job. I started to help, but handing me one of the biggest fish he said:

'Don't bother. We can manage all right. Go home and get warm and thanks for your help.'

I was grateful for the fish, but thinking how its species had defeated me, I felt I would have swapped a dozen like it for the satisfaction and joy of catching just a little one on hook and line.

*

One summer's day, with the holiday season in full swing, I saw a boy about eleven years of age sitting on the wall of the Albert Quay fishing. He had a bamboo rod, without a reel, his line just tied to its tip. He had a cork for a float. Alongside of him was a basket with a lid, a thermos flask, a half-eaten Cornish pasty and a half-skinned banana. He had bare, sunburnt legs, with sandals on his feet. He was wearing shorts and an open-neck cotton shirt. But for the thermos flask, the pasty, and the fact that his garments were beautifully clean and unpatched, it might have been myself of long ago. I sensed a kindred spirit.

But I felt sorry for him. Evidently he was a visitor. The Albert Quay was the last place any local boy would have chosen for fishing in the season, for it was the main landing place for small pleasure craft, as well as the ordinary harbour traffic. True, there were usually small pollack, the equivalent of our pennocks, swimming about the wall, but so many boats were tied to its rails that at present only a small area of surface water was visible, and it was impossible to see if there were any fish or not.

I watched him for a while. His cork float, although it kept moving horizontally in the slight swell made by the harbour traffic, gave no indication of a nibble. Then I said, with perhaps a suspicion of condescension:

'You know, you'll never catch anything here. There are too many boats coming and going all the time. If I were you I'd go down to Readymoney Cove, or go over to Polruan and along to the castle and fish from the rocks. There'll be no one to disturb you there, and sometimes you can catch quite big fish. I don't suppose you've had even a bite here.'

He looked up at me and smiled.

'Oh yes I have—plenty.'

'Have you? But have you caught any fish?'

He was still smiling.

'Yes—I've caught two.'

'*Have* you?' I said. 'Well done. What are they, little pollack?'

'I don't know what they are, but they're not very little. One of them pulled quite strong. They're in my basket.'

Without taking his eyes from the float he lifted the lid of the basket. Inside it were two mullet, one of them about a foot in length, both still quivering. I was astonished.

'Those fish are mullet,' I said. 'Do you know that I've been fishing here for years and I've never yet caught one on a hook? What bait are you using? Rag worm?'

'No. I couldn't get any worms. I'm using bits of banana. They seem to like it all right. Are mullet good to eat?'

'You bet they are,' I said, hoping there was no

bitterness in my voice. 'You bet they are.'

He lifted his rod, pulled in the line. The hook was bare. He put on it another pellet of banana and dropped the line in again. I said:

'Take no notice of what I said about moving to another place, my lad. Carry on.'

Since then I have tried fishing with bits of banana, with bits of orange peel, with dough, with mussel, worm, soft crab, maggots, ears of corn, trout flies and other artificial lures, but I have yet to catch a mullet on hook and line.

10

ALTHOUGH most of my fishing has been in the sea, I have at various periods fished in streams, rivers and lakes for trout, but never for 'coarse' fish, and never for the most desirable of all fresh-water fish, the salmon. I say 'fresh' because in British waters the salmon is rarely caught by rod and line except on its river migrations to and from the sea.

For one of these periods (and how I hated being out of sight and sound of the sea) I was living alone in a small isolated bungalow on the banks of the River Skirfer in the Yorkshire Dales. This river is one of the main tributaries of the River Wharfe. It is supposed to be the river of Charles Kingsley's famous book *The Water Babies.* Where it passed my bungalow it was a crystal-clear (and except in spate) shallow stream babbling over limestone ledges and gravel, with little waterfalls and deep pools. It swarmed with trout.

The fishing rights however were owned by an angling club and were strictly preserved and guarded by a water bailiff, who patrolled it day and night. Membership of the club was restricted and my application to join was peremptorily turned down. One of the pools was in sight of my front window; and on several occasions I had the tanta lising experience of watching one of the members whipping it with fly, and landing good-sized fish. His car, a Bentley or a Rolls, would be parked by my front gate.

I was hard up at that period, engaged on the writing of a book that just wouldn't come right, and otherwise extremely worried and unhappy, a state of mind for which fishing would have provided distraction, if not a cure. I had reason to dread the sight of the postman's red van coming along the road every week-day morning, stopping at my gate, the postman walking up the path with letters in his hand, so often one in the unmistakable envelope used by solicitors.

One day, however, there came a single letter which clearly was not, by its shape, a solicitor's. On its flap, in neat embossed black type was the legend Compton Place, Eastbourne. I had no friend or acquaintance with that address. It had been redirected from my publishers, my own name originally written by hand. It must be from a reader. It might be a 'fan' letter, a very pleasant change—unless like some I occasionally got it contained a sting in its tail, the writer, him or herself, having written a book and seeking criticism or advice about what publisher to send it to, a request which, in view of the admiration of my own work expressed in the early part of the letter, I could not refuse.

I opened it. It contained two closely handwritten pages, with the same embossed legend as the envelope. I glanced at the signature, the single word 'Devonshire' and read the whole letter with growing astonishment. It was from the Duke of Devonshire (not the present Duke, of course, for it was dated September, 1947). It began with an apology for 'a total stranger writing without a previous introduction'. My books had given him such tremendous pleasure that he would like to do something in return. He had read in one of them that I had never had any first-class salmon fishing. It would give him great pleasure if I would come and fish his bit of the Blackwater (County Cork) early next year. . . . What he would like me to do was pick a period of ten days, and I would be his guest. I needn't bother about tackle, he could lend me all I needed. He would do his best to be there with me, but if that proved impossible there was a butler who would make me feel not only at home but one of the family, a cook who would add quite appreciably to my weight during my sojourn. . . He could not guarantee any fish, but one of his friends this year had twice killed seven in a day, and there was still his own record of eight fish, averaging twenty-five pounds in one morning, to be beaten. . . . Finally, he hoped that I would accept his invitation in the spirit in which it was sent and accept it.

My first reaction to that extraordinary letter was to look out of my window, in the hope that I would see one of the Rolls-Royce anglers fishing in that, for me, forbidden pool, preferably the one who had rejected my application for membership of the club: to dash down, show him the letter and tell him he could keep his bloody trout. But it was late September, the local fishing season over.

And, incredible though it may sound, I had for various reasons to refuse the Duke's invitation. But at a later date, I met him by appointment at Brooks' Club in St. James's for lunch, the 'doorkeeper' giving me a rather haughty supercilious glance when I announced my name and business. I must wait until he had informed 'his Grace'. And he directed me to the cloakroom, although I had no overcoat or hat.

But there was none of this in the manner of the Duke himself. He took my arm, led me to a bar, and gave me a dry sherry which promptly dispelled my last twinge of nervousness. He was of medium height, of slender build, with a lean aristocratic face, with just a suspicion of bagginess under his eyes due possibly to an addiction to the port with which he plied me after we had done eating.

He was as genial as he had been in his letter to me. He pressed me to reconsider my decision about the salmon fishing, but was sympathetic when I told him in greater detail than I had done in my answering letter why I could not do so. We talked about fishing and fishermen and, slightly to my embarrassment, about the books I had written and the book I was still writing. I couldn't resist telling him about the forbidden trout river running past my door, which incidentally in the lower reaches passed through one of the Devonshire estates at Bolton Abbey.

When we parted at last there was a glow inside me that had less to do with the port than the encouragement he had given, steeling me for the next engagement I had to keep with a firm of solicitors in Lincoln's Inn Fields. I felt I could have faced the Lord Chief Justice himself and talked him silly.

The Duke is dead. Like the mullet, I still haven't caught a salmon with rod and line. But I have kept that letter and I will always cherish the memory of our meeting, not because he was a Duke and an aristocrat, but because he was a simple kindly man.

11

I HAD my first lesson in the art of fishing for trout with an artificial fly when I was about the same age as that boy who had caught the mullet on Fowey's Albert Quay with a banana bait. The circumstances were unusual. This was after the death of my beloved Captain Bunny. The *Lydia* had been sold to a Whitby fisherman. All the other summer pleasure boats had their 'boys', and anyway none of them had been launched down yet. It was before Whitsuntide.

There were two streams that ran down to the shores of the Bay. One was Stoupe Beck, near to which we had landed in the *Lydia* to wait for the sile to come in. The other was Mill Beck, a quarter of a mile nearer to the village and so called because there was a corn mill and farm about two hundred yards up from where it ran into the sea. And farther up from the mill was a dam, from which the water ran along a culvert to the water-wheel.

Both streams had trout in them. But Mill Beck belonged to the Squire, and there were notices along it to say that it was private and that anyone found trespassing or fishing would be prosecuted. The Squire was a big, powerful man with fierce eyes like a hawk's. What made these notices more frightening was that he was also a magistrate, and that if ever a poacher was brought up at the Police Court, he always did his best to have him severely punished. Not only that. I had heard that he had once caught a boy taking eggs from a pheasant's nest on his land, and he hadn't bothered to tell the police and have him prosecuted. He had thrashed him with a stick. I had been in the Mill Wood through which the stream ran above the dam many times bird's nesting, or looking for primroses or nuts, but I'd been careful not to be seen and I'd never really thought of fishing. For one thing the fish you saw in the beck above the dam were very small, smaller than pennock. They were shy, too, and always scurried under stones if you went near them.

Stoupe Beck had no mill or dam. It didn't belong to the Squire anyway, and although it was supposed to be private there were no notices to say so.

It was on a Saturday afternoon that I set off with my pennock rod and line, with no idea in my mind of trout fishing. I was going to try an experiment. Close to Stoupe Beck there was a scaur where the water was much deeper than those near the village, actually the very place where the Captain and I, when the tide had been high, had seen the huge shoal of billet. Although it was a fine day, an easterly wind was blowing, and when I got to the scaur waves were breaking where the water was deep and I knew it was going to be no good.

The beck was quite near and I walked up towards it, feeling very disappointed. The tide was down. When I got to the beck I had a surprise. Since I had seen it last there had been several storms which had stopped the coblemen from fishing. The waves had piled the shingle and sand, mixed with seaweed in the cove through which the beck ran and dammed it, making a long, deep pool which reached under a foot-bridge out of sight into the wood which grew on each side of the valley. The pool was muddy, with bits of seaweed floating on its surface.

But it was also ringed with rising fish.

I wasn't very excited. The fish must be trout, but one I saw jump clear out of the water was no bigger than a pennock, and I was thinking of the plaice and mackerel and gurnard, billet and cod, not to mention the scores of whiting we had caught in the *Lydia* not half a mile away that famous day. Still they were fish, and I might well have a try.

I knew that if you fished for trout you were supposed to have a licence which cost one and sixpence. That didn't bother me, for I didn't think I was going to catch one anyway. I'd just experiment. First I'd need an earth worm for bait. Limpets would be no good. I walked up the bank of the pool beyond the bridge which was nearly grown over with brambles. I turned over a stone where the soil was damp and soon found what I wanted, a small reddish worm, just the right size for my hook. I fastened my cork float about two feet above the hook, and not very hopefully cast it in. Almost instantly the cork went under. I raised the rod, and out came a fish, the first fresh-water fish I had ever caught on a hook.

It was about five inches long, bright as silver; with orange-coloured fins. It had no red spots on it as trout usually have, and it was long after that I learnt that it couldn't have been a trout, but a salmon parr, proof that real salmon had moved up the beck and spawned at one time or another. Even if I'd had a trout licence I would have been breaking the law by catching it. I put it in my bag, and looked for another worm. I soon had another fish, and went on like this until I had about a score, and really it was easier than pennocking. But they were all the same size as the first. I had seen much bigger ones in the Mill Beck, although even these didn't compare with whiting or billet. What pleased me most was to find how easy it was to catch them. I began to wonder whether the trout in the Mill Beck would go for a worm the same way if I crept very carefully near to one of the deep pools in the wood, so as not to scare them. The biggest pool of all, of course, was the mill dam. Dare I try?

I remembered that the Squire usually went to Whitby on a Saturday to attend the Police Court. It was also market day, and on my way along the beach I had passed the miller and his wife in their best clothes going to catch the train. I wouldn't have to pass the mill to get to the dam. I could reach the wood from the Stoupe Beck side. The more I thought of it the more I was tempted, and after one more fish, I wrapped my line over my rod top, walked back to the bridge, and started up the path on the other side. The fields on the top were level until I came to the edge of the Mill Beck valley. There was a cart road leading down to the beach. I crossed it and came to the edge of the wood. There was a notice here saying that trespassers would be prosecuted, but I didn't look at it. I went on until I was almost opposite to the dam. I could see the mill below me and to my right. Then I climbed over the barbed-wire fence into the wood and very stealthily moved down through the undergrowth until I saw the gleam of water. I stopped, with my rod flat on the ground, so that if I had suddenly seen someone I could have moved away from it.

The wood, deep in the valley and protected from the sea wind, was very quiet. The only sound I could hear was the cooing of a pigeon. I waited a bit. Then more cautiously than ever I moved down to a clump of hazel, from which I reckoned I would have a view of the whole dam as far as the wall. I squirmed on my belly the last few feet, and having reached the clump waited again and listened before raising my head and peering downwards. And then I had a shock. Just below me on the opposite side of the dam, half hidden in a clump of willows and sedge, was the Squire himself—*fishing!*

I had never been so frightened. I thought that he must have seen me, for he was not more than twenty yards away. But he hadn't. I lowered my head and started to squirm backwards, leaving my rod. I had scarcely moved when I heard a splash, and a sort of grunt from the Squire. I dared to turn and look and for a moment I forgot the danger I was in. The Squire had hooked a fish. His rod was bent, his line cutting the water from side to side just like a trolling line did when you hooked a mackerel. But why didn't he pull the fish in? Why didn't he get it to the bank instead of letting it play about?

It was my first lesson in real angling. It dawned on me that the Squire's line was very thin—I could scarcely see it—that he was drawing the fish towards the bank only gradually; for every time it gave a rush he eased the line out a bit, and reeled in when the rush slackened. The rushes were getting weaker too. The fish, although I could not see it, was getting nearer the bank. Suddenly the Squire bent down and picked up what I would have called a shrimp net, only it was round at the top, and the meshes were big.

He stepped forward out of the willows, dipped the net into the water and lifted again. I saw the gleam of the fish inside it. He took it out and I saw it clearly. I was disappointed. Although it was twice as big as any of the 'trout' I had caught it wasn't as big as a billet.

But the Squire looked pleased with it. He was

actually smiling as he put it in his basket and started to fish again. I was still well hidden in the hazels. I don't think he could have seen me if he had looked my way, and he was too busy for that. I wondered what bait he was using. He hadn't put on another worm when he had taken the fish off as I had done when I was catching my little 'trout'. Then as he cast the line out like the leash of a whip I saw a tiny black dot fall on the water. I saw that it wasn't a worm at all but an artificial fly, the same thing we had used for the billet except for its size and colour.

It had dropped near to where another fish had risen. He began to draw it slowly in with jerky movements, which must have made it look like a live fly. He didn't get another fish, and when it got near the bank he cast it out again. He went on doing this, and I thought how much more interesting this was than just throwing your worm in and waiting for the float to go under. Only of course you couldn't do it unless you had a proper fishing rod. Suddenly a trout plopped out of the water just under an overhanging branch on my side of the dam. The Squire saw it and cast his fly towards it. But instead of it falling on the water it caught on a twig of the branch.

He jerked it gently. The fly held fast. He went on jerking and then I actually heard him swear, for the line broke and dropped down limp to the water, with the fly still fast on the twig.

The branch was thin and the tree from which it grew had its roots on the edge of a low shale cliff which fell straight into the deepest part of the dam. I knew that the branch would not bear the Squire's weight if he tried to climb along it. He must have seen that too, for he took a small leather case from his pocket, and looked in it for another line. There could not have been one, for he put the case back, and then he tried to hook the loose end of the line with the tip of his rod. I felt really sorry for him as he went on trying, and I half wished we had been friends because I could have got it for him quite easily. Then, to crown it all he got the tip of his rod jammed between the fork of the two twigs. He jerked to get it loose and the top joint of the rod cracked as it came loose. He swore again quite loudly, which surprised me seeing that he was a magistrate and went to church every Sunday. But I still felt sorry for him. He must have felt awful, seeing the trout rising all over the dam, and not being able to go on fishing.

Yet I wasn't so really sorry when he took his rod to pieces, put it in a cloth case and moved away towards the dam wall from which a path led down to the mill, where I guessed he was going to call before he went home to where he lived, in a big house about two miles away.

There was no time to waste. As soon as he was out of sight I moved down to the tree, climbed the short bent trunk and swarmed along the branch until I was in reach of the line and the fly. It was easy to disentangle it. I swarmed back and got to the ground again, coiled it up and put it in my pocket. Then I made my way back to the hazel clump, picked up my rod and bag and moved up to the edge of the wood, where at the fence was the notice-board. I climbed over the fence, and at last I felt safe. I took the line from my pocket and examined it. It was of course not a line but a cast, not made of catgut like the snoods of our pennock hooks, but lengths of horse hair, knotted together. No wonder the Squire hadn't dared to jerk his fish straight out of the water. No wonder it had broken when he had tried to jerk it loose from the branch. It was about six feet in length. The fly had the tiniest hook I had ever seen. It was almost hidden by wisps of black feathers tied on with thin white cotton. It didn't really look much like a real fly. But then the Squire had kept moving it. The billet had never gone for the white feathers unless they'd been moving. Would the trout in the Stoupe Beck pool go for it as they had done for the worm? Should I go back there and try? It was a pity they were so small. Dare I creep back to the dam and have just one try there, just to see if I could catch one as big as the Squire's? By now he must have been well on his way home.

I looked at the notice-board and I thought of that boy who had been caught robbing a pheasant's nest, and what the Squire had done to him. It might be worse still if he caught me fishing in the dam. I would be taken to the Police Court, perhaps even put in prison. I hadn't done so badly anyway, with the trout I had caught at Stoupe Beck. Besides it was getting late. I put the cast back in my pocket and set off for home. But as I walked along the shore I couldn't stop thinking about the dam and the fly and I knew that I wouldn't be able to resist the temptation for long.

12

ACTUALLY I didn't wait longer than till Monday. The evenings were long, and after tea I set off along the beach. No one seeing me would have guessed I was going fishing for I had decided that my pennock rod was no good for fly fishing. I needed a hazel that was longer, more slender and whippy, and I had seen one in the very clump where I had hidden.

The wind was still east and the sea rough, and although the tide was down there was no one on the beach. I reached the Mill Beck cove, crossed the stream and walked up the lane on the other side. As I got opposite to the mill I saw the miller himself, his clothes covered with flour standing at the door of the mill, looking it seemed in my direction. He was a relation of the Squire, and just as tall and powerful, and he was as stern as the Squire about trespassers, but I wasn't trespassing yet, and as I had my hands in my pockets he couldn't have been suspicious. I was pleased to see him well away from the dam.

I went on up the lane until I was level with the top of the wood, and very stealthily now, got over the fence by the notice-board and moved down to the clump of hazels. I could see the dam. The fish were rising, too, snapping at flies that were hovering close to the surface. I cut the longest of the hazels and trimmed it smooth. I knew it was no good trying to fish from this side of the dam, because of the trees. I moved on up the wood until I came to where the beck ran into it, and the water was shallow. I crossed over to the other bank. But there I stopped for a while, listening. The pigeon was cooing again, but there was no other sound except that of the plopping trout.

I was a bit frightened, but also very excited. I tied my pennock line to the thick end of my new rod, twisted it round until I got to the tip, then knotted it again, leaving about six feet over, and to the end of this I tied the Squire's cast and fly. I listened again then tiptoed along the level bank as far as the willows until I came to the gap in them where the Squire had stood. I could see his footprints in the soft mud.

The trout were rising all over the dam, but the water was so muddy I could only see those that jumped out for the insects. I stood as near to the edge of the bank as I dared—it was very slippery—and made a start. I soon discovered how difficult it was to throw a fluffy fly and a light cast straight out, so that the fly would drop clear. Instead of this it went into coils, which fouled the fly. The Squire's rod, of course, had been much longer, and he had used it almost like a cabman's whip. All I could do was to shorten my line so that only the cast was hanging from the tip and hold the rod out as far as it would go. That wasn't far and I couldn't jerk it along through the water as the Squire had done. I began to wish I had just got my pennock hook and float, and could fish the same way as I had done at Stoupe Beck, with a worm for bait. I decided I would do this after a few more tries with the fly. And it was then I got a dreadful fright. I heard voices and the snapping of twigs above me in the wood. I crouched down in the willows. The sounds drew nearer. I dared not look to see who it was. There was no need, for one voice was the Squire's and the other I thought was the Vicar's. They must have come to fish. I was trapped.

They stopped not more than ten yards away from me on the wall end of the dam. I could hear every word they said. I hadn't known that the Vicar went fishing, although I knew that he sometimes went shooting with the Squire when he wore ordinary clothes except for his round collar. He was supposed to be a very kind man. He was rich and he used to send parcels of food to the poor people of the village and grapes from his own greenhouse to the sick, even to those who didn't go to church but went to chapel. But he was strict and stern and I had always been afraid of him. Even if the miller and the police sergeant had been with the Squire now I couldn't have been more frightened. And to make things even worse I heard the Vicar say:

'You are right about the place being full of fish. Quite big ones by the look of it. You can't have had any poachers this year.'

And the Squire answered:

'No. It's not the local people who do it. It's the visitors who have no respect for the law. Fishing with worm too. I actually found a set line here one day, with half a dozen hooks on it. But the miller keeps a sharp look out for anyone coming up the road or down through the wood. I've given the police constable the tip too. There's some very nice fish. They grow at a great rate here in the dam where there's plenty of food for them. You'll have to watch out for the trees though, on the far bank. I lost a cast last time I was here.'

There was a silence during which I supposed they were getting their rods ready. I wondered how long it would be before they found me and what I should say, for I didn't see how I could possibly escape. If I tried to run they would hear me, and I was sure that with his long legs, the Squire would catch me before I got very far, and that would show that I knew I was guilty. It wouldn't be so bad if he didn't know that I had been trying to fish: if I said I was bird's nesting, or looking for flowers, only there weren't any flowers near the dam and it was long past daffodil or primrose time. If only I could hide the rod and the Squire's cast and fly. . . .

They had started fishing. I could hear the whip of their rods. I looked at my own rod. I thought that the best thing would be to cut off the cast and line and bury them in the mud, then push the rod into the willows out of sight. I got hold of the thick end and started to pull it towards me. And then an extraordinary thing happened. I had left it with the fly just dangling out of the water. I must have made it jerk so that it looked exactly like a live fly, for a trout bigger than the one I had seen the Squire catch, leapt out and grabbed it. I felt a tug on the rod itself.

For a moment I forgot the peril I was in. I just couldn't help doing my best to catch that fish. I drew the rod in till I came to the cast, and then hauled and the cast was stronger than I had thought, seeing that it was only horse hair. I saw the fish just below the edge of the bank, its head out of the water. I was on my knees. I leaned over, made a grab at it, jerked it up on to the bank. And as I did so I lost my balance, slipped over the edge into the dam waist deep, saving myself only by grasping one of the willow roots. As I dragged myself out, I saw the Squire striding towards me, the Vicar close behind.

They must have seen the fish, flapping on the bank. The Squire looked mad with rage. He seized me by the arm, shook me:

'Poaching, eh ? You young devil. What do you

mean by it? Setting a line too.'

I was crying, for apart from the Squire I'd had a bad fright falling into the dam. The Squire shook me again.

'What do you mean by it?'

I couldn't speak. I thought he was going to start thrashing me. But then the Vicar, who looked stern but not quite so angry, stepped forward and put his hand on my shoulder and he said to the Squire in quite a gentle voice:

'Don't harm the lad. He's only little. Perhaps he didn't know he was doing wrong. We've all been young once.' And to me he said, more sternly: 'Don't you know it's wrong to fish here, setting a line? You could be taken to the Police Court for doing that.'

I found my voice at last: 'Please, sir. I didn't set a line.'

'Then how did you catch that fish?' the Squire said.

The Vicar bent down to look at it, and before I had time to speak again, the Vicar actually laughed. He pointed to the fish.

'Why—look at it,' he said to the Squire. 'It's got a fly in its mouth, and a horse-hair cast. Look, there's the rascal's home-made rod. He must have caught the fish fair at any rate.'

The Squire let go of me. He bent down and looked at the trout. And then he said in not such an angry voice:

'Where did you get that fly and cast, boy?'

I thought it best to tell him nearly the whole truth, not mentioning that I had been fishing first at Stoupe Beck. I said I had been in the wood on Saturday because it was too rough to fish in the sea. I was looking for flowers really when I had seen him fishing. I had seen him catch one trout and then get his line caught in the branch. I would have got it for him if I hadn't been afraid of his being angry about my being in the wood. I just wanted to see whether I could catch a fish with a fly myself, that was why I had come to the dam today. I wasn't really fishing when the trout got on. It was an accident, but once it had got on I couldn't help hauling it in. I didn't want to keep it, of course.

I dared to look the Squire straight in the face then. Both he and the Vicar were laughing, and the Squire said:

'Well, I'm blessed. Did you ever hear such a story? Using my own gear to catch my own fish. And a very nice one too.' And then he said, sternly but not angrily: 'Now be off home and get your wet clothes changed or you'll catch your death of cold in the east wind. And don't let me catch you here again or I'll put a stick across your bottom.'

I said: 'Thank you, sir,' and I started to go, but he told me to stop. He got hold of the trout, took the fly and the cast from it, and handed it to me.

'Here, take your fish. But don't forget. No more poaching or trespassing.'

13

DURING the years I have acquired a certain skill in the conventional mechanics of fly fishing. You use your rod like a stock-drover's whip, flipping it backwards and forwards to give the line impetus, then on the forward stroke let it go. But I have had limited opportunities for putting this into practice. I am assured that there is excellent trout fishing in the River Fowey. The licence fee is reasonable and there are few restrictions. But the attractions of estuary and sea have always been too strong. Besides, the gear is expensive, and just before my return to Cornwall from Yorkshire I had given my one and only surviving fly rod and reel to a young friend of mine who was going to live in Alberta. It was a beauty, built by a famous firm. I had bought it at a sale, and never had a chance to use it.

Undoubtedly the trout is among the aristocrats of fish. It will live only in the cleanest waters free from contamination, although in streams and rivers it thrives on the normal discolouring earthy dirt brought down by heavy rains, for this contains worms and the larvae of insects. It is a beautiful fish to look at and, of course, delicious to eat. Its sight and hearing are acute. If the water is clear, you've got to stalk it, cat-footed, and when hooked it fights like a fish twice its weight and size.

Trout fishing, and certainly that of my choice, too, is usually found in sylvan surroundings or among mountains or lonely moors, so that if the fish prove elusive you have the many other aspects of nature as a compensation, especially in spring or early summer when the fishing is at its best: the beauty of the landscape, the singing of a lark, the cry of a curlew or nesting plovers, the sight of a water-ouzel, speeding up- and down-stream or perched on a rock, wagging its tail, then diving for a caddis grub, into the very pool where you are bent on catching your fish.

In the early years following the end of the First World War, when I was struggling to earn a living as a writer, there was a little book published by *The Field* called *Where to Fish,* which, fulfilling its title, listed hundreds of places in the British Isles where every sort of fishing was available: with information about licences, permits, close seasons and accommodation for anglers, from posh hotels with private waters to ordinary lodgings.

That volume was enough to drive any angler of limited financial resources mad, especially if he happened to be living in a bed-sitter in London's West Kensington and the month was April with spring in the air. But the sale of a short story made it possible for me to flee London and take lodgings in the Devon village of Chagford for a week and fish for trout in a moorland tributary of the River Teign, for a fee payable to the Duchy of Cornwall of, I think, half-a-crown. I didn't catch, nor did I see, a single trout in the stream and apart from the wild beauty of Dartmoor, reminding me of my native moors, what I remember most of that fishing holiday was the Devonshire cream, and blackberry jam and new-baked 'splits' my landlady put on my table for every meal.

At another time I stayed at lodgings in Lynmouth and fished with moderate success among the rocks and boulders of the lovely River Lyn, that river which when the walls of a reservoir burst in a heavy rain swept down and engulfed the little township in an unprecedented disaster. There was a summer when, inspired by information I had read in *Where to Fish,* I took lodgings at a farm in Yorkshire's Commondale where trout fishing was available in a tributary of the River Ure. But this happened in the year of a record drought. After two days of unsuccessful fishing in that stream it dried up completely; yet again I had the beauty of the countryside to console me, and if there were no cream and blackberry jam splits at the farm, there were lashings of Yorkshire ham and eggs and home-made Wensleydale cheese to remember.

Lake Ullswater, in that tantalising volume, was strongly recommended for its trout. As I had never previously visited the Lake District I fell for the bait one year, staying for a fortnight at a holiday boarding house in Patterdale, at the south end of the lake, and the foot of Helvellyn. Although it was too late in spring for Wordsworth's daffodils, 'nodding their heads in sprightly dance', the lake, with its surrounding fells, justified all that I had read about its romantic beauty, but I had no luck whatever with the trout.

One day I decided to climb Helvellyn. It was not really a climb, for there was a well-used path leading from the village all the way to the top. It was just a matter of jogging up and along, stopping now and again to admire the magnificent views. The weather was fine, hot and windless. Short of the top I sighted on my right, and not more than a hundred yards from the path, a small tarn, and above it some derelict buildings which I guessed belonged to a disused mine. I climbed down to the tarn and was astonished to see on its smooth surface the rings of rising fish. They were trout but very small. It looked as though they had been put there as fingerlings by some fishing enthusiast.

I returned to the path, and I was still short of the top when I sighted another tarn, this time on the left, and much bigger. Again I investigated. Again there were rising fish but this time (and some of them were leaping clear of the water) they were big ones, at a guess at least three-quarters of a pound. Why—oh why—hadn't I brought my fishing gear? There were no forbidding notice-boards. There was no sign either of any human beings. I was tempted then and there to go back to the village, get my gear and climb up again.

There were still a few days of my stay left, however. I carried on to the top of Helvellyn with my appreciation of the view only slightly damped by thinking about those trout and the opportunity I had missed, for by this time I had learned that there is no fish more temperamental and elusive.

I set off early next morning with a packed lunch. The weather again was fine and hot, without a breath of wind. Again the trout were rising in the tarn, leaping for flies hovering over the dead-calm surface. By all the rules, the really expert trout angler should be an entomologist able to identify the insect on which the fish are feeding, and to select from his fly-case the appropriate artificial imitation, each of which has a name. And of these there is an immense variety, as indeed there is an immense variety of British insects although to the average non-angler the insect world consists only of those which sting or bite, like wasps and midges, or household pests like bluebottles and spiders, or those beautiful to look at, like butterflies.

I was not an expert angler and I was not an entomologist. I had about twenty flies in my case, and the only ones I knew the names of were Black Gnat, May Fly and March Brown. Black Gnat closely resembled the one the Squire had used and lost and I had pinched on that dramatic episode of the Mill Dam. As it was the month of May, my May Fly might have seemed to be an appropriate choice, certainly more so than the March Brown, but the insects hovering over the tarn looked more like ordinary midges which are, of course, a variety of gnat. I put on my Black Gnat.

In spite of what I had learned from the Squire, I hadn't much faith in a horse-hair cast. I was sure that it would break with a really big fish. I had instead an eight-foot length of what was then known as Japanese gut, the forerunner of the synthetic-gut substitutes universally used today. My line was pleated silk, my rod split cane (nothing like the beauty I had given away), but one which I had acquired second-hand, made by a reputable firm. I had the misfortune to crack the middle section, and had mended it with splints and a tight whipping. I had a landing net.

I started to fish, confident that at last I was in for some real sport, and under ideal conditions. Perhaps one of the most agreeable of these was that I had the tarn and the whole of Helvellyn for that matter to myself. But the trout showed not the slightest interest in my Black Gnat, although time after time I successfully dropped it in front of their very noses. I changed to the May Fly, thinking that although there were no real May flies about it might tempt one as a change from the midgelike insect that they were taking so avidly. They ignored it. I went on until I had tried almost every fly in my collection, without success. My wrist and arm began to ache and I had to rest. I sat down and opened my luncheon parcel.

While I was eating I became aware of a change in the weather. The sun was still shining, but it had lost its brilliance. High up a thin veil of mist was forming over the blue of the sky. The fells to the east were losing their sharp contours. The air was becoming closer. My theory that the trout were feeding on some species of midge or gnat was confirmed when I felt the pests on my face and the back of my neck and my bare arms. A cigarette was only a partial defence against their attacks. The fish were still making rings on the otherwise glasslike surface of the tarn. Was it because of its very calmness and clarity that they would not take my fly?

I picked up my rod again and changed the fly back to the original Black Gnat. Then as I made my first cast, I heard the sound of distant thunder coming from the west. The horizon in that direction was hidden by the mountain summit, silhouetted against the partly veiled sky. Through that veil was visible the sharper edge of a dark cloud rising and moving east. There was another peal of not-so-distant thunder.

I was alarmed. To be caught in a thunderstorm near the summit of one of England's highest mountains would not be a pleasant experience. The chance of being struck by lightning was remote, the odds considerably greater than winning a fortune on the football pools, yet lightning was one of the well-known hazards of mountain climbing. I had better pack up and hurry down the path while the going was good. Yet I hesitated, for suddenly, and I knew it was further evidence of an approaching storm, there came a gust of wind from the east, ruffling the surface of the tarn. I saw a trout jump clear from the water not six yards out. I cast. There was a swirl where the fly had dropped. I had hooked my first fish. I landed it, and cast again, and again I hooked a fish.

For the time being I became oblivious to the weather. It might have been the ruffling of the surface causing my fly to be less distinguishable from the live ones, or it might have been because it had blown the live ones away, but the trout had gone mad. With every cast there was a swirl where the fly dropped, as though not one but several fish had seen it. Some I missed and had to cast again. Some I hooked and lost before I netted them. But I had more than a dozen good fish when I was dazzled by a flash of lightning, with a peal of thunder that seemed to shake the ground. Then came the rain in an almost solid vertical wall.

It was soon, between the lightning flashes, as dark as dusk. All I could see was the tarn, boiling with the rain, and its immediate surroundings, and the beginning of the rough path, down which I had come from the main path that led to the mountain top. I dismantled my rod, glad that it was not a steel one like the mountaineers' ice-picks which sometimes are struck, and set off up that path taking the extra precaution of keeping my rod horizontal with the ground, for the lightning was now almost continuous, although because of the rain I could not see the actual flashes and only judged their proximity by the time lapse between flash and thunderclap. They were near enough!

I reached the main path. It had become a rivulet, which however left me in no doubt as to its direction. It had occurred to me that I might find shelter in one of the mine buildings above the other tarn. But I could not see them, nor the tarn itself. I plodded on and down, soaked to the skin, my eyeballs aching with the flashes. The path was slippery and I was wearing shoes with latex soles. Time after time I fell flat on my backside.

And then as suddenly as it had started the rain stopped. The sky began to lighten. I saw a patch of blue to the west, extending swiftly eastwards. The summit of Helvellyn, well behind and above me, cleared, and as I watched, it was as though a huge billowing sea of snow was being rolled away from the landscape, revealing the lake and fells, all suddenly lit up by the sun. And beyond, from the eastern horizon, mounting halfway up the sky, was the solid mass of storm clouds, gleaming white at their summit and almost black below where the rain was still falling and lightning flashed.

It was magnificent, a sight, like those daffodils of Mr. Wordsworth, to remember. But my delight in it was mingled with a strong sense of relief that the storm had passed without using me as a lightning conductor, that I was now at least halfway down the mountain path towards my lodgings and dry clothes, and that I had, by the weight of my bag, the proof that trout couldn't always fool me.

14

THE moorland hills in which Bramblewick's two becks have their source form a watershed. They slope down to the west into a valley through which runs another beck, one of the sources of the River Derwent whose ultimate outlet is the Humber. Although this valley runs almost parallel with the main coastal motor road and at its nearest point is less than a quarter of a mile away from it, few motorists would guess its existence. Even in the height of summer when the road traffic is continuously heavy, you can wander along it and never meet a living thing except the black-faced moorland sheep, a covey of grouse or maybe an adder. The noise of the traffic is mellowed so that it is like the sound of the sea.

The beck in its early stages, and in dry weather, is scarcely more than a trickle. Here and there, however, where in floods it has carved out the peat, there are deep pools, big enough to harbour fish, and in one place, more distant from the motor road, a wall has been built across its course, forming a tarn about half the size of the one where I had fished so successfully on Helvellyn.

The tarn had been made by a rich man who had leased the sporting rights of the moor from the Lord of the Manor, some years before the Kaiser's war. He had done it with the object of attracting wild ducks and teal, especially in winter time. He had also stocked it with young trout.

As a boy, and as a young man (up to the outbreak of war, when I enlisted), I had on many occasions tramped over those moors, which although the game was strictly private were regarded as common land. One of the moor's main attractions to me was that it abounded with tumuli and other relics of Early Britons. Wherever the heather had been burned, and the turf removed for fuel by the farmers who held turf and sheep grazing rights, you could by careful searching find flint implements: scrapers, knives, arrow-heads and, near the tumuli, even bits of ancient pottery and beads.

But I had also on many occasions tried fishing in the beck, first of all with worm, later when I had acquired a real rod, and the necessary skill, with fly. Worm had proved useless, for those deep pools swarmed with minnows (never found in Stoupe or the Mill Beck) which took the bait the moment you threw it in. With fly the biggest trout I ever caught was scarcely bigger than a pennock.

I had of course seen the tarn. I had seen trout rising in it. Unfortunately not more than a quarter of a mile away was the cottage of the gamekeeper, whom I had passed several times on the open moor, a big rough looking fellow with an unfriendly face, always with a gun under his arm. So far as I knew he had never seen me with my fishing gear. But he always eyed me suspiciously.

It was on an evening of July in the year 1934, with 'the war to end all wars' ended, but with another in the making, that I set off with the deliberate but not particularly hopeful intention of fishing in that tarn, which I had not even seen for so many years. I had heard on good authority that the War Office was taking over the whole of the moor as an artillery range and battle-training ground. The lease of the shooting rights had expired. The crusty old gamekeeper was dead and his cottage unoccupied. So far as my informant could tell me, and he was a young farmer who lived near the moor and grazed his sheep there, there were no fish left in the tarn which was mostly grown over with weed.

He had never seen anyone fishing. I was then temporarily domiciled in Whitby six miles away. I rode out on my push-bike. The weather was cloudy but dry, with a moderate westerly wind.

The main road now was busier than ever, with touring coaches and a regular bus service running between Whitby and Scarborough. In places it had been widened and some of the sharpest corners straightened out. But once over the wall (where I left my bike) the moor seemed just as it had been when I had first seen it as a lad. The heather was thick, already starting to bloom and exude its nostalgic scent. I hadn't gone far when a cock grouse got up at my feet and sped off cackling indignantly.

I was following a winding sheep path, always a favourite place for finding flints. I kept my eyes open for them. I came to a tumulus and couldn't resist having a look round it where the sheep had trod the ground bare. I picked up one flake of flint which might have been the beginnings of an arrow-head, rejected by its maker, whose remains, together with his weapons and possibly some pottery once containing food, might be entombed in that mound of earth and stone.

I moved on towards my goal, as indeed that man of the ancient past might have set out on a hunting or a fishing venture with bow and flint-tipped arrow or spear, and I came to the edge of the valley. I stopped and looked down at the tarn. My first reaction was one of dismay. Except for two small patches, one near the wall, and one at the middle it was entirely grown over with weed. If it did contain fish it would be impossible to use a fly except in the clear patches.

But as I looked I saw that the patches were changing shape. Most of the weed was duckweed, floating on the surface. Only at the shallow end where the beck entered were there rooted aquatic plants. The duckweed was moving in the wind, which although light was blowing in fitful gusts, but predominantly down the valley towards the wall, where the clear patch was narrowing while the one in the middle of the tarn grew bigger. But it was still only a patch, and well out of casting range from the shore. Nowhere was there a sign of fish. It looked as though my best chance of proving if there was anything alive under the water would be along the dam wall. I walked down towards it and near its end, sat down in the heather and rigged up my gear. It was the same rod I had used on the Helvellyn tarn, and as it had proved so deadly on that occasion I put on a Black Gnat, with a cast—if not the same one, similar—of Japanese gut.

Leaving my landing net with my haversack, I walked halfway along the wall and made a start, dropping the fly wherever I could see clear spaces among the duckweed. I went on along the wall casting the whole way to its other end, then moved gradually back. The tiny fronds of the weed were sticking to my line. I had stopped to wipe them off when out of the tail of my eye I was aware of something moving nearly in the middle of the tarn just short of the clear patch. I looked hard in that direction. Something *was* moving, stirring the surface of the water, and definitely it was not the wind. It might be dab-chick or some other diving bird. It might be an otter, in which case it would be good-bye to my fishing. I should know when it surfaced.

I reeled in my line and hurried along the edge of the tarn until I was opposite to the clear patch. Nothing had surfaced, and now there was no sign of movement either. I stood waiting, wondering if I had imagined it or if it had been some trick of the light. And then I saw it again among the duckweed at the edge of the patch, something moving slowly just under the surface raising little waves. Suddenly its speed increased. There was a swirl in the water and I caught just a glimpse of a dorsal fin. *It was a fish,* and by the size of that fin a mighty big one.

My heart was beating fast. I did my best to keep calm and measure up the situation. The patch of clear water, and it was only relatively clear, was at least twenty yards from the shore. Even with the wind behind me I could not cast half that distance. I must either wait for the fish, which had disappeared again, to come within that range, or wade in the same distance. I didn't know how deep the water was. When the fish had made that sudden rush, obviously it had been to seize some sort of moving prey. There were no visible insects on or near the surface, because of the wind. Perhaps it was feeding on minnows, or tadpoles, which lessened my chances of hooking it with a fly.

Should I wait? I'd be lucky indeed, if it moved in within casting range into water clear of the weed. And it would be dark within another couple of hours. I saw its bow wave again, almost in the same place, not in the clear, but near enough for it to see my fly if I could drop it there. It was now or never. I took off my jacket, whipped off my shoes and socks, rolled up the legs of my trousers and stepped into the water, which near the bank was quite shallow with a hard stone bottom, only thinly covered with soft peat.

But the proportion of peat to hard ground increased with every wary stride I made from the shore. It was soon well over my knees. Shortly I discovered that the bottom was giving way to pure peat, a thick spongy mass which must have made the bed of the original valley before the dam was built. I needn't have troubled to roll up my trouser legs. My feet sank through the peat. The water soon was almost waist deep.

I had learned the technique of bog and mud walking from my many wanderings over the moors. No matter how deep it is and how soft there is a point at which it compresses sufficiently to give temporary support for feet so long as you keep moving. What bothered me was that when I did come within range I would have to stop and stay put if I were to use my rod.

It was hard going. With every stride I had to extricate one foot from the peat against its powerful suction, leaning my hand forward on the other leg. Yet I was making progress. Another half-dozen strides and I would be near enough to cast. I struggled on, the edge of the clear patch at last not more than four yards away. And then fortune favoured me. My foremost foot encountered something hard under the peat. I explored it with my toes and found that it was a boulder, broad enough and flat enough to give me, when I got my other foot on it, secure support.

All this time I had seen no further sign of the fish. With my feet planted on that providential rock, and the water no higher than my knees I dared to stand up straight, doing this slowly, for nothing startles a fish more than sudden movement. I looked towards the place where I had seen it last. There was no sign of it. The wind was still blowing, not as before in gentle gusts, but in all directions, one moment in my face, next on the back of my head, and with every gust the area of clear water changed shape and size as the duckweed moved.

I kept my rod low, the fly in my left hand, ready for the first sign. And then it came, not where I had seen it last but at the most distant margin of the weedless patch, the bow wave, moving slowly, and almost out of range. But the wind temporarily was with me. I let go the fly, pulled out a length of line from the reel and began to whip it out, with every backward stroke increasing the length, with the fly itself well clear of the water. First forward, then back and forward gaining in distance each time. And then with what I knew to be the limit in capacity of my rod and skill, I let the fly drop, short by at least six feet of my target. As it began to sink I gave it a gentle jerk. There was a sudden swirl in the water. And it was as though electric current had passed through the line and the rod from the invisible fish to me. The miracle had happened. The fish was hooked. The battle was on, and by the strength of that current I knew it was going to be a tough one.

I hadn't got its full weight yet. The line was taut, but it was evidently moving only slowly, puzzled to find that its movement was restricted. I braced myself for what was coming. I had to make sure that the hook was well home. I gave the line a jerk, relaxing it instantly by lowering the rod tip, and it was as well I did so, for the line tightened as a fiddle string as the fish panicked, whizzing the line from the reel as it shot off straight down the tarn towards the dam wall. I didn't try to check that rush at first, but as I watched the reel the terrifying thought came to me that there was only fifty yards of line, and that I had never taken the precaution of looking at the knot which tied its end to the spindle. I mustn't let the last coils out. I must check the rush before that happened.

I pressed one finger against the spinning reel. I raised the rod, until I got the full weight and strength of the now kicking fish. The tension on the line was so great that it vibrated and made a high-pitched musical sound like a fiddle string. I hung on desperately. Either the line or the rod must break unless I could relax the strain. I did the only thing possible. I stepped off the rock back to the peat, holding the rod horizontal. But as soon as my feet sank in I saw that I could not follow the fish. I would have to keep moving, but it must be in the direction of the shore where I had first stepped in and I would have to move backwards.

The fish was still kicking, the line still vibrating and making that extraordinary sound. And then as I was groping for the next backwards foothold, the line suddenly went slack. I raised the rod. There was no resistance. Certain that the fish had broken free I began to reel in. I hadn't got half of it in when I saw the line itself move sideways, cutting the water. The fish was still on. I raised the rod just in time to take the strain of another rush, this time not from the direction of the dam wall but from the opposite shore, to which it had swung round.

The reel started to spin. I checked it slightly with my finger, then near the danger point gave it full check and hung on. Again the line sang. Yet I had a feeling that the tension was not quite so great as before, and I attempted another backward stride, more difficult than ever, for I must have sunk up to my knees in the peat, the water being up to my waist. I dared not for one moment take my attention from the line. The fish had changed direction again. It was keeping near the surface, still only distinguishable by its 'bow wave'. At each turn I was able to gain a little line, and I began to hope that gradually I would be able to manoeuvre it in towards the shore.

My progress was slow, but continuous. The shore was getting nearer, and in spite of its rushes, and its kicking, I was certain the fish was tiring. I was gaining the line too. I was still in the peat however, still striding backwards. And I was still in the peat, with one foot, and the other raised and balanced for the next stride, when the fish charged, not away from me, but straight up the line between me and the shore. I swung round maintaining my balance by a miracle. I actually saw the fish as it passed me, or at least I saw its tail. The line of course was slack. Frantically I reeled it in, it was coming back, even nearer to the shore. The line was still slack as it passed me, and to tighten it I raised the rod, foolishly either too suddenly or too high. It took the full weight of the fish. It bent and, at the point in the middle section where I had spliced it, snapped, the top coming down almost to the butt.

But the fish was still on, and I still had the rod in my hands with the shore not more than a dozen feet away from me. I faced it, and with both sections of the rod gripped tightly in my hand moved towards it. I reached the hard ground. My next two strides brought me to the shore edge. I turned and then dropped the rod so that I had the line only in my hand. I could feel the weight of the fish, but it wasn't kicking. I started to haul in very gently, wading back towards it as I did so, but keeping on the hard ground. I halted when I saw the knot of my cast. Then slowly I began to move shorewards again, inching the line in ready to let go at the first sign of another rush.

There was less than a foot of water at the shore edge. Had my landing net been there instead of fifty yards away, the rest might have been simple. Dare I try to coax the fish along the edge of the tarn until I came to where I had left the net? With my rod intact I might have done it. But I had left the net well up the bank among the heather. I would have to leave the line in order to get it. My only hope now was to get it close into shore, land it by hand.

I went on gingerly hauling. I came to the knot, to the cast and still the fish was offering no resistance. And then I saw it not more than half the length of the cast away, and it was moving in as obediently as if it had been a well-mannered dog on a lead. I had never seen a trout so big, even in a glass case. It was more than two feet in length. A cannibal trout, possibly the one survivor of those which had been put in the tarn soon after it had been made so many years ago.

I was still in the water, close to the low bank. It came in until it was almost at my feet. It was now or never. I coiled the slack of the cast round my left wrist. It was immobile with only its gill slits quivering. I bent down, lowered my hands, one on each side of it, just short of the head. With my fingers extended and curved like the talons of a hawk I moved my hands deeper and nearer until they were almost touching. Perhaps they did touch for the tail jerked. What happened next was reflexive. I closed my hands, gripped with all my strength and lifted it out of the water. I swung round, got one foot on the bank, slipped and stumbled, but as I did so I flung it forward on to dry land, and as it dropped pounced upon it. It was kicking still, only a yard from the water. I took it in my arms, and with my broken rod and line to which it was attached trailing behind, I rushed up the bank until I was at least twice the range of a jumping salmon, and dropped it safe among the heather. And it was only then as I looked at it exultantly, that I could really believe that a miracle had happened. That here indeed was the big fish that didn't get away.

15

IT has so happened that, with intervals of war service and foreign travel I have spent several years of my adult life domestically unattached both in my native 'Bramblewick' and Cornwall. I can only refer, with diffidence, any reader who may be mystified by that remark to certain books which I have written (available if all else fails in the Reading Room of the British Museum) in which he may find a clue if not a completely satisfactory explanation.

These books with one or two exceptions are autobiographical novels. They are based on my own experience, written in the 'first person', but in them, exercising 'poetic' licence, I have frequently departed from the literal truth, giving fictitious names to people and places, inventing dialogue, even incidents, juggling with time, advancing it here, retarding it there and, like an artist, painting a picture, heightening the lights, deepening the shadows in keeping with my instinctive conception of what the finished picture should be. Truth and time are only relative.

But this, I can assure the over inquisitive reader, is not so with the present volume except perhaps in its chronology, in its irrelevant omissions and in the names of people and places I have written about in my novels. The name Robin Hood's Bay is a mouthful, and I always thought it slightly phoney, for even if Robin did exist, there is alas not the slightest evidence to support the legend that on his death-bed, with Friar Tuck, Maid Marion and Little John in attendance, he shot an arrow into the air to mark the place where he was to be buried, and it fell on the highest point of the Bay moor, where actually there is a tumulus, known as Robin Hood Butts. Some bow, and some arrow if he shot it from Sherwood Forest!

Bramblewick may be equally phoney, yet blackberries are called brambles in this part of the world. South along the coast is a small hamlet called Hayburn Wyke. Wyke is a terminological variation of Wick, and as Bramblewick rolls easily off the tongue, I prefer to use it. Likewise, I am calling my fishermen friends 'Lunns' although their real name is Duke, and the real name of 'Fosdycks' is Storm, of Scandinavian origin, for although they were the old-timers of the village they were the descendants of Norwegian fishermen who came to the district when Whitby was one of the principal ports for the Arctic whaling industry.

Close to the onset of the industrial slump which followed on the temporary boom at the end of the Kaiser's war, still a bit groggy from the after effects of a jungle crash in which I had miraculously escaped from being burnt to death, I went back to Bramblewick. I'd had little success as a writer. London had got on my nerves. But my strongest motive for returning was a nostalgia for the things I had loved as a boy, the old village itself and its folk, the sea and the scaurs, the woods and moors, but above all the fishing. It was late autumn, when the codling and even cod feed close in to the shore on the flood, and fishing was at its best from the scaur ends at low tide, from the cliffs, when the tide was high.

I had been awarded a war disability pension on

my retirement from what during my service had become the Royal Air Force. I had rented a small furnished summer letting cottage at only ten shillings a week. I had enough to live on with what I might earn from writing.

There had been many changes since my boyhood. Some years before the war four families of fishermen lad emigrated from Flamborough, thirty miles south along the coast and settled in the village. At that time only two cobles were engaged in year-round fishing, both manned by surviving members of the Fosdyck family. They undoubtedly resented the coming of the 'foreigners' but it had its compensations. The daily task of hauling up the heavy cobles in winter time was now shared. The lifeboat, with Luke Fosdyck, eldest of the family, now coxswain, had a professional crew.

Among the 'foreigners' the youngest was Henry Lunn, with a family of two school-age sons and two daughters, with more to come. Now, after the war, there were again only two families left fishing, the Fosdycks, Luke, Tindal and Oliver, and Henry Lunn with his grown-up sons, John and Marney. During the war both sons had served in the mercantile marine. The other surviving 'foreigners' had gone back to Flamborough. Henry had been given command of a decked motor vessel, known as a 'mule' fishing out of Whitby although he hadn't moved his family. There was then a boom in fishing, with so many men and boats on war service. The owner of the mule however had sold it when the war was over. With his sons back home he had invested in a new coble, but this time one equipped with an engine, which meant that it was considerably heavier than the Fosdyck's for hauling.

But I was not at first particularly interested in the

activities of the fishermen. I was too involved in my own troubles, bothered in particular by my failure to achieve any real success as a writer (I had a growing collection of editors' rejects). You could have called it an inferiority complex. And the antidote, the anodyne if not the cure was out on the scaurs, not when the cobles were coming in with their catch, but when they were deserted at dusk or nightfall or by the light of the moon.

My gear was simple. A stout seven-foot sea rod, with what is known as a Scarborough reel six inches in diameter, so that it can be hauled in fast. A hundred yards of light but very strong flax line, no trace, and a single short-snooded hook attached to a short brass boom two feet up from the four-ounce sinker: my bait lug worm, rag worm, 'peeler' crab or mussel. The crab or mussel being soft would have to be bound on to the hook with thin cotton. My favourite bait was rag worm.

Getting this bait was itself a pleasant and diverting occupation. At low water on a spring tide, there were in the creeks between the scaurs, flat pieces of shale only lightly attached to the bed rock. In parts they were not attached at all so that there were spaces under them giving shelter to marine animals, gobies, starfish, brittle stars, baby urchins, hermit crabs, sometimes tiny lobsters, as well as the rag worms, which were bigger and tougher than those found in mud. 'Rag' was an unfortunate name for them, for they were handsome creatures, not unlike a millipede in shape and in their multiple equipment of tiny 'legs'. But they were reddish brown in colour, iridescent, their heads furnished with a pair of retractile claws. Their more appropriate scientific name was *Nereis pellagica,* suggestive of a water nymph. The fishermen did not use them because unlike the lethargic lug worm they were extremely mobile, difficult to impale on a hook.

My choice of fishing ground depended on the weather, the state of tide and condition of the sea itself. If the tide was out the best time to start was dusk just before the tide turned, and one of the best places the West Scaur of the Landing, close to the farthermost post, where the water except at the lowest of spring tides was deep.

I can see it now, as though time had stood still, and I was there. I can smell the sea mingled with the ozone exuding from the carpet of weed covering the scaur. It is still only dusk, but the lights of the cottages perched on the cliff edge beyond the shore end of the Landing are coming out one by one. There is no wind. The sky is overcast, the sea grey and formless except where about fifty yards out there is the gleam of broken water where the waves of a gentle ground swell press shorewards.

I have brought a candle lantern, but there is enough light yet for me to take one of those wriggling rag worms out of my bait tin, and put it on the hook. With my rod raised in my left hand, my right hand on the reel, I adjust the weighted end of the line so that it is suspended from the rod tip half the length of the rod, bring it behind me, swing it up and forwards gripping with both hands, but with the fingers of the right hand pressing the reel, and at the critical moment letting go so that the sinker and bait make an unimpeded flight until they hit the water when I check the reel to stop the line over-running.

I have cast well out and seawards of the scaur towards where the underwater jungle of tangle begins, but just clear of it, where there is a patch of shingle. And now I must wait for the turn of the tide when, if all goes well, the codling will start to come in and I will get my first bite, and perhaps my first fish. In the meantime I am imagining them in large numbers, lurking among the tangles, waiting as I am waiting, then one of them more impatient than the others, swimming in towards that patch, nuzzling the shingle for little crabs or anything else eatable, seeing or perhaps scenting that wriggling worm, snapping at it. . . .

I don't hold the rod in my hands, which although there is no frost in the air are coldish, and if I let them get numb, I will find it difficult to handle the bait. There is a notch in the post at a convenient height from its base. I have rested the rod in it with its butt on the ground and its top leaning forwards. The rod tip is furnished with a white porcelain ring still easily visible in the growing dusk. My eyes never leave this ring. The slightest movement of it will mean a nibbling fish—a jerk and I will have the rod in my hands for action.

If the tides are neap I may have to wait half an hour for the turn. In that time I will have hauled in once or twice to make sure that my bait hasn't been taken by crabs and although I am wearing two extra sweaters and a thick greatcoat, with thick fishermen's stockings inside my rubber thigh-boots, I am getting more aware of the cold, even with my hands in my pockets. Darkness has fallen. I have lit my lantern, placed it so that it shines on the porcelain ring.

At last the rod jerks. I forget the cold. I seize the rod, feel the tugging fish, strike, wind in, and there it is splashing in the water at the scaur's edge gleaming in the light of the lantern, a codling too small to need the gaff, but a fish and a nice one. And from then on, for perhaps half an hour with a neap tide and until the water is lapping the bottom of my lantern, I am catching fish as fast as I can re-bait and cast. If they are spring tides then it may be only ten minutes before I have to move on to another place, but rarely give it up altogether unless I am too cold to bait. . . .

This was one of the periods in my life when fishing had become an obsession. I could scarcely think of anything else, least of all work. Yet looking back I can see that this in itself was a sort of self-healing instinctive physiotherapy. If I couldn't concentrate on writing I was concentrating less on my misfortunes. Fishing was a narcotic; but even carried to excess it produced no hangover.

The Landing was only one of several places where I could fish, but all of them had the disadvantage that when the tide was flowing (and it was no good on the ebb) you had to keep moving to another. The Rocket Post Scaur where as a boy I had caught the big eel was one of them. If I'd been fishing at the Landing however until the tide had caused me to move it would be some time before it was high enough here, and I would move on south along the shore to Mill Beck, where with a scaur to fish from, there was a stretch of sand leading out well beyond low water.

On this sand, which was Bramblewick's most popular summer bathing beach, I had sometimes as a lad caught flounders when the tide was very low, using an iron rod as spear, wading along with bare feet until I trod on them, then driving the spear down. Although I was now fishing for codling there was always a chance of hooking a flounder. Yet it was the fishing and not the fish that was the narcotic: the anticipation and not the fulfilment.

That and the peace and solitude of my surroundings, with no sound in my ears but that of the waves, no smell but that of the sea.

When the tide was high, spring or neap, the place to fish was the Gunny Hole Nab. This was at the north end of the village lower down from the row of cottages built along the cliff edge. Here was a bluff, forming a narrow cove where once there had been a narrow slippery path giving access to the shore when the tide was down. The bluff was about thirty feet high. At its seaward extremity there was a small level place reached by walking along a precarious ridge of shale. There was just room on this level place for a firm and safe foothold when casting, and space for lantern and gear. The sea-bed was all smooth shale, with only a few patches of bladder wrack, so there was no danger of your hook fouling. Unlike the Landing, there was no waiting for the fish to come in a shoal on the turn of the tide, giving only a few minutes before you would have to move. The procedure was the same, except that the rod would be leaned against a forked stick instead of the notch in the Landing post. The fish, if there were any, were solitary ones, but as a rule they were bigger, so that even if you were sitting down the rod had to be within inches of your grasp.

There was a night and a particularly cold one when after a long wait during which there had been no sign of fish, I was obliged to respond to a call of nature, not simple seeing that I was wearing an extra pair of trousers under my ex-officer's greatcoat, that my hands were numb, my legs shaking a little with the cold and that I was standing less than two yards from the edge of the bluff. It took me some time to find what I was groping for. Successful at last, I was not more than halfway to the complete fulfilment of the operation when the rod was jerked off its support. I swung round just in time to grasp its butt as it slithered over the cliff edge, knocking over my lantern as I did so.

For a moment I did not dare move my feet. I was in pitch darkness and in grasping the rod I must have got very near the edge. One step and I might be over. I pulled the rod in however, raised it, found the line slack, and started to reel in until it suddenly tightened, and I felt the furious kicking of a fish. Only then, with my eyes getting accustomed to the dark, dared I take a backward stride to safer ground, when I crouched down on one knee.

The fish was fighting. I just hung on, recovering my wits, for I'd had a fright. The strongest swimmer could not have survived for long in the cold dark sea below the Nab. But the fish helped to restore my confidence. I started to reel in very slowly, checking only at its most vigorous kicks, hanging on, not giving it any line. At night, with the lantern illuminating only a circle of ground around it, it was impossible to tell exactly where the sinker had fallen from a cast for its splash would be out of sight and hearing. I shouldn't know now where the fish was until it reached the cliff bottom and the line became vertical instead of slanting out.

No landing net or gaff would be of use then. It would be a straight haul, against its dead weight, up the vertical face of the cliff and then over the edge, which was rounded and slightly overhanging, so that even with the lantern I could not have looked down it.

But the angle pull was steadily decreasing. There were a few more kicks, when I just hung on, and then came that change of weight which warned me of the climax. I stood up. The rod bent, for it had now become like the jib of a crane. There was no more kicking, yet I hauled very slowly, taking one very careful step nearer the edge to keep the line clear. I knew it was coming near, that it was just under the overhang. I did not dare risk a sudden lift. With the reel checked I took a backward stride, put the rod down, got hold of the line and pulled in. The fish, just vaguely visible, slithered over the edge, up the little slope and on to level ground. I pounced upon it with one foot, held it firm while I fumbled for my matches, and lit the candle in my lantern. From the way it had pulled and the fright it had given me, it should have been at least a four-pound codling. It was a billet, an overgrown pennock, weighing not more than a couple of pounds. But for once having caught a fish I had no desire to go on fishing.

I completed the operation the fish had interrupted, removed the hook from its mouth, and as I had no desire for a fish supper, didn't like billet anyway, and it was still alive and unharmed I heaved it over into the sea, where but for the grace of God I might have been myself. I packed up for home.

16

SNOW came early in December, with a squally northeaster and a rough sea which kept the fishermen ashore. It was only a light fall, chiefly of hail, but as there was a moderate frost it lay, transforming with a new beauty the appearance of the old village and the countryside, a beauty that I found still more exciting late one night when, with the moon full I set south along the shore for a place where before the war I had often fished successfully.

The gale had blown itself out, leaving a heavy ground swell. The tides were spring, but the gale had retarded the ebb so that the Landing would have been no good. Besides the seas were still breaking across its mouth. Mill Beck would be no better. As so often happened in rough weather, the waves had scoured most of the sand away leaving instead a thick mass of torn-off tangles washed in from deep water. This I had discovered on the morning ebb when I'd been out on the scaurs for bait. I had the very slender hope that I would find conditions better where I was going. Anyway, it was a night of splendour, with the moon riding high in a cloudless velvety sky, its light so brilliant that every detail of the sea and the scaurs and the snow-clad land stood out sharp and clear. The offshore sea, no longer torn by the gale was deep purple, its waves glinting only as they rolled in towards the scaur ends to curl over and shatter into foam as white as snow. The roar of them was continuous. It echoed from the cliffs through the still frosty air, as I made my way along the beach, past Mill Beck cove, then to Stoupe Beck, where south of its valley, the cliffs began their gradual rise to the massive headland of what I prefer to call High Batts.

The contours of that headland had always made me think of a gargantuan recumbent lion, with its head erect, its forepaws reaching out to sea where the cliff foot terminated in a rugged scaur, covered by the sea only at high tide. I had seen it in many moods; its summit clad in purple heather, quivering through the heat on a summer's day: I had known it with a bank of fog obscuring its top for days on end when the Bay itself was bathed in sunshine. I had seen it lit up by the sun as with a battery of searchlights, silhouetted against a background of dark thunderclouds: but never had I seen it more exciting than as it appeared now in the light of the moon and the glittering stars with the snow on its top, and edging the dark shadows of its crags.

Southwards of Stoupe Beck the scaurs ran in parallel lines with the cliff, but between the cliff foot and the nearest of them the beach consisted of loose wave-rounded pebbles that made walking difficult. I kept to the scaur, but remembering the pebbles, that the scaur would be submerged on my way back, I had put on a pair of light ankle-boots instead of my heavy rubber waders. As it was I was wishing I had dispensed with my greatcoat, for I was wearing two sweaters and an extra pair of jeans. I was walking fast, and in spite of the frost I was too warm for comfort. It was important that I should arrive before the tide turned. I still had half a mile to go.

Short of the headland itself the steepening cliffs curved inwards to form a little bay. Here there was a geological fault so that the scaurs, like those of the

Landing ran out in a seaward direction, the outermost forming a sort of breakwater against the swell resulting in a relatively smooth area of water closer in to the shore. This was my objective, what was virtually a lagoon enclosed like the Landing by two scaurs, one known as the Billet Scaur much higher than the other. It was wide and deep at the abrupt end of the high scaur but narrowed sharply into shallow water and the shore which here was smooth, weedless shale.

I saw it as I rounded the bluff of the bay, and at first glance I felt hopeful. Although the waves were pounding on the outer scaurs, the lagoon seemed calm enough. The high scaur was bare to its end with what seemed to be about three feet of freeboard between its edge and the surface of the water. If the tide hadn't turned, it should be at least half an hour before it rose over the scaur obliging me to move.

I reached the shore end. From the shallows it reached out about fifty yards. But as I walked along it, I saw that the water, although its surface was calm, was rapidly moving outwards, like a river, that where it had been shallow the shale was now bare. I hadn't reached the far end when this movement was reversed. The shale was inundated again, the level of water, rising rapidly up the scaur edge. It dawned on me that although the waves were not breaking close in they were producing with their back-wash a powerful surge. There was less than a foot of 'freeboard' at the scaur end when I got to it, and almost immediately it began to recede again.

I had never fished here before except in summer and in calm weather. It was a favourite place for billet. I remembered an occasion when at dusk the lagoon was packed with herring sile, driven in by the bigger fish, not only billet but codling and horse mackerel. They were leaping out of the water in their frenzied pursuit of the sile. They went as madly for the fly I was using. With every cast I hooked a fish. Thinking of the long walk home I was selective, putting back all the horse mackerel, which although lovely to look at are too boney to eat, and all but the biggest of the billet and codling. At other times I had caught good-sized flounders, once a sole, and although I had never had a really big fish, there had rarely been an occasion when I'd been completely unsuccessful. And now I had never felt less hopeful.

I took off my greatcoat, folded it and put it down on a dry part of the scaur, for I was sweating with the thickness of my garments. Even my hands were warm and I had no difficulty in baiting the hook. I made my first cast, not a long one, for beyond the scaur end the tangles grew thick, and I could even see the fronds of them when the surge made its seaward movement.

I rested the rod on my greatcoat, its tip projecting just a short way over the scaur edge, and I lit a cigarette. My vigil had begun. The minutes passed. Soon I was aware that the tide had turned. The inward surges were perceptibly rising higher up the scaur, and not receding so far. I was not so warm now. My feet were getting chilly, and not daring to move from the rod, I began to stamp on them, to restore the circulation. The frost I was sure was increasing in intensity. Even my hands were feeling cold, although when I'd finished my cigarette I had thrust them in my jacket pocket, my warmer trouser pockets not being available because of those extra jeans.

Some sort of action became imperative. I hauled

in, and rather to my surprise found the bait gone. I re-baited and cast again. Thinking that my greatcoat would be of more use if I put it on, I laid the rod flat on the scaur. But as I reached for the coat, the rod tip jerked. I picked it up, felt a fish, reeled in and landed a small codling. I unhooked it and threw it back.

This was action at least. I didn't bother about my coat. The bait was still on. I cast again, this time holding the rod in my hand. At once I got another bite, another fish the same size, too small to keep, and this time only a bit of the bait remained on the hook. My fingers were getting numb. The cold seemed to have no such effect upon the wriggling rag worms in my bait tin. It was a devil of a job, seizing one, holding it between thumb and finger-tip, and with the hook in my other hand impaling it.

As I cast again it was with the thought that I would have to give it up very soon and not wait for the flood tide to drive me off the scaur. One more fish, perhaps two if it was a bigger one, and I was through. I waited, holding the rod in my hands, stamping my feet on the scaur. The bite did not come. I would count up to fifty, then fish or no fish, give it up. I counted. Nothing happened. I raised the rod, to tighten the line and raise the sinker from the bottom. And I got a tug that made me gasp. It was a fish, something really big.

It was moving seawards. If it got among the tangles I would lose it for certain. I gave it a little line, then checked and hung on while my rod bent dangerously. The fish did not yield an inch, but it started weaving. There was nothing I could do but just hang on until there were signs of it tiring. Then I must work it gradually in to the scaur edge within range of my gaff. But I was aware that those inward surges from the breaking rollers were now reaching perilously near the edge of the scaur. In a few minutes they would be lapping over it. There was no time to play it, to give and take. I would have to risk the rod or the line breaking, and simply haul it in. Holding on grimly with my left hand I started to reel. I hadn't made a complete turn, when I found it would not move. The line had jammed between the standing part and the moving part of the reel. It couldn't be freed unless the reel was dismantled, and the fish was still fighting to break loose.

I hung on. A surge brought the level to the very edge of the scaur, and there was actually a wave moving in, not high, but enough to show that the outlying scaurs would soon cease to act as a breakwater. Unless I could shorten the line it would be impossible to bring the fish close enough into the scaur for me to use the gaff. There was only one course left. I must drag it up the length of the scaur into the shallow water at the inner end of the lagoon, and hope for the best.

I looked for my gaff. It was near to my bait tin a yard or so away from my greatcoat, and hanging on to the rod with my right hand only, I managed to seize it and hook it into the breast pocket of my jacket. I'd have to come back for the coat. With both hands on the rod now, I began to move backwards up the scaur, dreading, but expecting that with every stride I took the line would break. Not for one moment did the strain on it and the violent kicking relax. I was gaining only the length of my strides.

Before I was half the way up, there was a surge that lapped over the scaur and over my ankles. I stopped until it receded, leaving the scaur bare again by at least a foot. There was no time to lose. I dared to move faster, almost resigned now to the certainty that the line must break before I reached the shallows, for there would be no shallows once the real waves came in. And it was a wave that brought the next surge, not breaking but bigger and flooding over the scaur and moving ahead of me into the shore. At that moment the line went completely slack. I raised the rod, saw that the line was actually moving in with the surge, but still with no pressure on it. Then came the back-wash, the reverse surge, baring the shale at the end of the lagoon. Close in to the shale, in less than a foot of water was the fish gleaming white in the moonlight, lying on its side, flapping.

Another and still bigger wave was coming in. I leapt off the scaur into the water. I reached the fish, saw that my line was still attached to it, although still slack. I took no chances. I gaffed it and dragged it shorewards, with the wave rising above my knees. It receded, leaving the shale bare again, but I moved on until I was almost at the foot of the cliff, well clear of the next wave. And it was not until then that I dared to stop and look at my prize.

It was a magnificent cod, as big as any I had seen landed by the fishermen in the old days, weighing I guessed at least twenty pounds, the biggest fish I had ever caught. It was still kicking. I stunned it with a stone. Then remembering my coat, I dashed back to the scaur, temporarily bare again, ran along it and saw the coat washing in with a wave which, although I was on the scaur, came over my knees. I grasped the coat with my completely numbed hands, and dragged it up the scaur as soon as it bared. It was as heavy as a suit of armour. And when I reached the fish again I was presented with a problem, not made simpler by the fact that I was now shaking with cold, my feet as well as my hands numb.

I was nearly three miles from the village. With the tide flowing fast covering the close-in scaur I would have to walk along the pebbly beach as far as Stoupe Beck. By the time I reached Mill Beck the tide would have reached the Nab. I would have to cross the beck by the foot-bridge, climb the steep path, slippery at all times and now covered with frozen snow, to the cliff top and then along the cliff path, and down again to the village. The fish was too big and heavy to carry with my hand. I would have to sling it on to my rod and carry it over my shoulder, and there was my soaked and heavy greatcoat.

I couldn't afford to lose my coat, and I'd be damned if I'd abandon my fish. There was only one way to carry the coat, and that was to put it on. I made it into a heap, stamped on it to squeeze some of the water out. With the extremest difficulty and discomfort, for it seemed that the sleeves had shrunk, while the cuffs of my jacket and multiple jerseys had enlarged, I got it on. I slung the fish over my shoulder. Its wetness could make little difference to the wetness of the coat already penetrating my inner garments. Then, trying not to think of how warm I had been an hour ago, and only of the comforts of my far-off home I took my first staggering stride towards it.

17

APART from the two families of fishermen, there were few able-bodied men left in Bramblewick. Long before the war a new coastguard station had been built (of ugly brick) on high land above the village. There had been six coastguards with a chief officer when I was a boy, all reservists from the Royal Navy, the men wearing Jack Tar uniforms, the chief the uniform of a petty officer. In those days the life-saving rocket apparatus, with its wagon was kept in a shed close to the watchhouse, and every quarter the coastguards, with a volunteer company, would have a practice on the beach, pretending that the post on the Rocket Post Scaur was the mast of a wrecked ship.

It was always done with the tide almost covering the scaur so that a man could wade out to the post along it, yet with deep water between it and the beach where the apparatus was set up. The rocket attached to a long thin line would be fired over the post so that the line would drop near to it. Then one of the coastguards, not in his usual uniform but in canvas 'fatigue' clothes would wade out, pick up the line and haul in the thick double rope on which the breeches buoy would travel. Attached to this rope was a block or pulley, and also a little board on which was printed in several languages instructions to the supposed shipwrecked sailors to fasten the block as high up on the ship as possible.

The coastguard would climb the post and make

the block fast. He would wave his hand as soon as he had done this, and the men ashore would haul out the breeches buoy until it reached him so that he could get his legs into it and leave go of the post. Then to us lads would come the most exciting part, for the rope would lower with his weight as he was hauled in and he would splash into the water, pretending at least that it was too deep for him to walk. He had to pretend too that he was unconscious when he got to shore. He was carried up the beach, and several of the company in turn would practice artificial respiration on him, pressing up and down with their hands on his chest.

There was now only one coastguard left in the 'new' station, a middle-aged ex-petty officer, whose duties were to hoist the Union Jack on the flagstaff every morning and lower it at dusk, to hoist the storm-signal cone when he received instructions from the District Officer at Whitby (by telephone) to do so; to keep a special look out in bad weather and fire the gun that summoned the volunteer 'rocket' company in an emergency. The apparatus and the practice post were now on the cliff top. The old coastguard station, which, with its watchhouse, made one of the two ramparts of the village against the sea, had been bought by the Universities of Leeds and Sheffield as a marine biological laboratory. It was closed throughout the winter. Most of the fishermen's cottages too had been bought by city dwellers, occupied only in the holiday seasons. The lifeboat was still in its house, but threatened with removal, for it needed more than a crew to launch it on its heavy carriage down the steep slipway and haul it up again, even in fair weather for a practice mission.

It wasn't long before I realised how hard it was

for the two surviving families of fishermen to gain a living from the sea. Their chief problem was the hauling up of their cobles, impossible without some mechanical device. They had rigged up a capstan, like that used on old sailing ships for hauling up the anchor. It was a thick oak post, rotating on a heavy iron pinion cemented deep into the metalled surface of the Dock in line with the slipway. It was furnished with four long arms. Pushing these round wound in the hawser attached to the coble carriage, very slowly, but more or less efficiently, how much so depending on the number of helpers manning the arms. Naturally I would be one of them if I happened to be there, and not down on the scaurs getting bait for my own fishing.

I gathered later when I got to know the Lunn lads better that they had thought that in the early days I had been a bit 'stand offish'. They had been seamen, and although serving in the Merchant Navy in the war, subject to discipline. I had been an officer, and although I was a civilian again they had presumed I couldn't forget it. Besides, I talked la-di-dah. Also they had thought (and perhaps they had some justification for this) that I was not quite right in my head, messing about the scaurs all day long, fishing at all hours of the night, cold nights, too, when anyone in their senses would be at their firesides, keeping warm.

We were anyway on speaking terms, and I had observed that whenever I did give a hand with the capstan Henry Lunn never failed to say 'thanks'. More than once he had offered me a codling, which I had tactfully accepted, even when I had fish of my own catching in my larder. The Fosdycks would not have dreamt of such politeness and generosity. Yet while I did not like them I had always admired them, especially old Luke. They were all big powerful men, masters of their craft, absolutely fearless, indomitable in their unending encounters with the dangers of the sea. They were gruff, unfriendly, yet never actively quarrelsome. They were possessive, yet they had accepted the pre-war 'invasion' of the Flamborough fishermen without protest, although it meant a sharing of the local fishing grounds. There was a brotherhood among the fishermen of the coast, to which they too belonged.

But they were of an older generation. Luke, who had succeeded Matt Cooper as lifeboat coxswain, was now in his sixty-fifth year and due for retirement. Tindal was only a year younger. Oliver was over fifty, with greying hair. Luke and Tindal were childless. Oliver, who had married a 'town' girl who had come to the village as a mother's help with a summer 'visitor' family, had a grown-up son who resolutely refused to follow his father's profession and had become an assistant shopkeeper.

Henry Lunn was in his prime, still under fifty. He was short in stature, broad shouldered, strong and active. The Fosdycks were dark. He was fair with blue eyes, and a bristly almost gingery moustache. He had good teeth and a pleasant smile. The two sons were also short, but of the two John was the heavier in build, slow in his movements and speech, inclined to a gloomy outlook on life. Marney was slender, wiry, quick in his movements, and as I was to discover, quick witted, humorous, audacious almost to the point of recklessness, supreme in the craftsmanship of his profession. Both were blue eyed with fair hair.

Not surprisingly, I had slept in after my heroic, arduous, moonlight journey along the beach and the cliff top. I needed the sight of my gigantic fish lying on a newspaper on the living-room table alongside my typewriter, the pages of an uncompleted story, and the crockery of my last meal to convince me that the whole adventure hadn't been a dream. But what should I do with the monster?

I was getting tired of the taste of fish for my meals. I had weighed it before gutting it. It was just short of twenty-one pounds, enough to feed a small multitude. There was a fishmonger in the village, but he got his supplies from the Fosdycks to whom he was related. I mustn't crash in on their market, and anyway I must not set up as a rival professional.

I had no milk for a meal. I walked down to the Dock hoping to see the milkman at the end of his round. Both cobles had been hauled up. It was freezing hard, but there was no wind and it was clear that with the swell falling away the fishermen had been out. I was just in time to see the Lunn brothers, carrying a basket of fish between them rounding the corner of the lane that led to their warehouse. Still a little diffident, I followed them. The door was open. Henry was there, loosening the nails from the lid of a fishbox. He smiled and said:

'Now, then. It's a nice morning.'

The brothers had started to pack their fish into the box. Without looking up John said:

'It's a bloody cawd 'un if you ask me.'

'Nobody did,' his brother remarked. 'You've always got summat to complain about.' He turned to me and said good naturedly but with a faintly detectable sarcasm:

'I didn't see you out on the Landing Scaur last night. Was it over rough for you?'

I had the feeling that the ice was breaking. I said:

'The tide didn't ebb low enough. I went on to the

Billet Scaur.'

'That would be a tidy walk,' said Henry. 'Did you catch owt?'

It was a polite enquiry, and I was embarrassed. I didn't want to give the impression that I was boasting. I was watching the packing of the fish. They were all codling, not one more than six pounds, and with the basket nearly empty, the box was still not full. I had best be frank.

'Yes. I had a bit of luck. I got a cod, a big one.'

John looked up.

'How big?'

'I think it's round about twenty pounds,' and I added hurriedly, 'it's no good to me. All I wanted was the fun of catching it. Would you like to take it with your own catch ?'

'We'd buy it from you,' Henry said quietly. 'We've had only a middling catch oursens. I can't tell you how much until we hear what this lot brings. Where is it? Can you fetch it afore we nail the box up?'

I said firmly, 'Yes. But I don't want paying for it.'

He laughed. 'Have it your own way. Let's see it anyway.'

I turned to go, and John said. 'A twenty-pound cod? Eh, you're not kidding us are you?'

I didn't answer. In a few minutes I was back with my fish. Henry was the first to speak.

'By gum that's a good 'un. Bigger than any we've had this winter. Do you mean to say you got it on your rod and line?'

They were hard-bitten professional fishermen. They wouldn't be interested in, or impressed by the dramatic details of how I had landed it! The surge, my numbed fingers and feet, the jammed reel, the wave that had miraculously deposited the fish on to the shore, my struggle with the soaked greatcoat, the walk home. I said:

'Yes. I had a bit of a fight, of course, and a bit of luck too.'

Then Marney said, still sarcastically:

'It strikes me we'd better go in for rods and lines oursens, and give up coble fishing.' But he added without sarcasm, 'It's a good fish. I bet it pulled.' And then, 'Eh—why don't you come off with us one of these days? It might change our luck.'

I didn't know whether to take him seriously. In all my years in Bramblewick I had never been to sea with any of the coblemen. Nor had I even in summer, seen one of them taking 'passengers'. This would have been cutting in on the trade of the pleasure boatmen.

'Do you mean it?' I said.

'Aye. Why not?' he answered.

'It *might* change our luck,' John put in gruffly.

'What time will you be off tomorrow?'

'Round about seven—afore daybreak,' said Henry, implying his assent. 'That is if the weather stays like it is, and it doesn't start to blow again.' And to his sons, 'Don't fill that box tight. With that big 'un what you've got left will do for another box.' And finally to me, 'If you won't take brass for it, think on, there'll be a codling for you whenever you want it.'

The ice was broken.

18

THE men were already at their cobles when I got down to the Dock. There had been no change in the weather, except that the frost had increased in intensity. There was no wind. The sky was cloudless, the stars shining brighter with the moon down. There was only a murmur of surf from the Bay. The only other sound in the still icy air was the footfalls of the men, and then the creaking of ropes, the crunching of wheels on the frozen snow as they moved to launch the Fosdycks' coble. None of them spoke. It was as though they were engaged on a military operation against an unsuspecting enemy, fearful of giving the alarm.

The tide was ebbing but still only halfway down the slipway. I was the amateur, willing to help but not knowing whether to pull or push as the boat was moved to the slipway top, and then down to the water's edge. The carriage wheels were chocked then, the coble heaved forward until the bow was in the water. The carriage was withdrawn, swung round against the watchhouse wall, the coble was pushed until she was half afloat, and with one man climbing on board, and at the oars, was given a final push. The other two returned to help with Lunns' coble.

So far no one had shown any sign that they were aware of my presence. But as soon as the bow was awash and the carriage withdrawn Henry said laconically:

'Jump in now if you're coming.'

I got in, moved up to the bow. The men pushed, and as she floated jumped aboard. We moved past the other coble as she backed in for her crew. Henry was already in the stern fixing the rudder and tiller. John had taken the lid off the engine, and was priming the two cylinders. He gave the starting-handle a swing. There was a splutter and then a silence, during which the other coble moved past us with two men at the oars, and John started unscrewing the plugs for another priming. They were four lengths ahead of us, when after a vigorous swinging the engine started. John closed the lid. Marney with a cigarette already in his mouth offered the packet to his brother and to me. And as we rapidly overtook the Fosdycks, I heard him say in a low voice to John:

'By gum, I thought you were going to let them have the laugh on us, like that time you'd forgot to fill the petrol tank.'

I had no doubt that by 'them' Marney was referring to the occupants of the other coble, a hint of a rivalry between the two families. Despite that they were helping each other it was inevitable that the Fosdycks should feel jealous of the Lunns' engine. But John, who clearly was the 'engineer', merely retorted:

'Anyone can do that. And I didn't expect it to start first swing, a frosty morning like this.' And to me he said: 'What do you think of it, eh? More than twenty years old, and running like a Rolls-Royce! We got it second-hand, and all she needed was new main bearings!'

Certainly it was a good engine. The other coble was soon far behind, just visible in the starshine and the light reflected from the snow-bound land. We were nearing the outer post of the West Scaur, the coble easily riding the long rollers of the swell. It was too deep here for them to break. We passed the post. Henry swung the tiller round so that we were moving south, and Marney said:

'Eh, father, what's the idea? Are you thinking about the Billet Scaur and that big cod he caught?'

Henry laughed.

'We might as well end up there,' he answered. 'We'll start shooting at Mill Beck, and keep along the scaur ends. It's as good a spot as any, with the Fosdycks shooting to norrard from the Landing, as they're bound to do, with them having no wind to sail.'

The coble was much smaller than the Fosdycks'. With the lines each coiled on a wicker tray called a skep, piled round the engine box, the only free space was in the bow, where I was standing. As yet I wasn't feeling undue discomfort from the cold. I'd had a good breakfast, ending with a mug full of hot coffee. I had my dried-out greatcoat, my thigh-boots with two pairs of stockings, and had taken the precaution of putting on another woollen vest, with an extra pullover under my jacket. So far I was enjoying the experience of being water-borne, feeling the rhythmic movement of the boat over the slow swell, the companionship of these so likeable men. They were wearing yellow oilskin buttonless smocks; the sons with caps on their heads, Henry with an old felt hat.

We were nearly opposite to Mill Beck, now about a quarter of a mile from the shore, where at low water of a spring tide the outer scaurs would be bare. There was a perceptible greying of the eastern seaward sky, a dimming of the stars. Suddenly Henry gave the order.

'Right. We'll make a start. Throttle your engine.' Marney had lifted the first skep level with the gunwale. He threw the buoy over, and as soon as its warp was tight, he followed with a small grapnel and started the shooting, throwing the baited hooks clear, the coils of the line following. There were, although I didn't know it then, four hundred hooks on each line, spaced a fathom apart, each hook with a two-foot cotton snood. The bait was mussel, and as the shooting went on and the light in the eastern sky increased I could admire the dexterity with which Marney picked up each baited hook from the pile on the skep in its right succession, and had the next one clear before it was in the water. We were moving at least at half speed, twice as fast as a heavy coble would have done with two men pulling at the oars.

We were opposite the Stoupe Beck, when with the skep nearly empty, John lifted the next one, knotted the line to the free end of the first, and as Marney shot the last hook removed the empty skep and put the other in its place, so that there was no break in the shooting.

We were now on the very ground where on that warm summer day of long ago Captain Bunny and I had fished in the *Lydia,* hauling in the whiting and gurnard and plaice, two at a time and I observed that Henry was altering course shorewards so that the second line would cover the ground. He was I was sure, banking on a few flatfish at least, although I knew it was rare that the coblemen landed them in winter.

I was thinking of that summer's day as I felt the cold gradually penetrating my multiple garments. My feet, in spite of the two pairs of stockings I had put on, were already numb. Had I been rock fishing, I could have stamped on them, moved about.

Besides, whenever the cold, measured against my desire to go on fishing, reached a certain point of discomfort I could give it up for the warmth of my cottage fire, and a hot drink. Here I was trapped and it would be hours yet before we returned to the shore. There were still four lines to shoot.

Were my companions completely indifferent to the cold? It looked like it. Their hands were bare, and Marney's fingers certainly could not have been numb the way he was handling the baited hooks, and any doubts I might have had were dispelled when Henry, looking towards the seaward horizon now streaked with pink, remarked:

'It looks like being another nice day. Sun's coming up red, and I've yet to have it proved that a red sky at daybreak means bad weather.'

'Nay,' put in John. 'But that doesn't mean we're going to get owt like a catch.'

'Don't be so bloody gloomy,' Marney said. 'Think of that big cod he caught at the Billet Scaur. Where there's one there might be a score.' And to me he shouted: 'Eh, where was the tide when you hooked it, ebbing or flowing?'

'Just flowing,' I answered.

'Well, we're as likely to get 'em on the ebb.'

We had made a wide circuit of the sandy grounds and Henry was steering direct for High Batts Point. The third line was bent on. The seaward sky now was suffused with a more vivid pink, and suddenly out of the sea came the edge of the sun itself, rising slowly, at first elliptical then full circle as it cleared the horizon. It was a deep coppery red. It threw a line of tinted light along the smooth, undulating surface of the sea. But the most spectacular manifestation of that light was on the shore. The cliffs and, in particular, the precipice of

High Batts, which had been almost black in contrast with the snow-clad fields and moors above them glowed as though they had been carved from solid burnished copper, making an even more startling contrast with the snow. It was superbly beautiful, exciting like the curtain rising on the first scene of a Wagnerian opera.

With the third and the fourth and the fifth line shot and the sixth bent on we were drawing near to High Batts. The redness of the sun, still low in the sky, was changing to a harsher dazzling light so that Henry had to keep holding one hand to the brim of his hat as he steered. He had altered course. We were moving closer to the shore, on a line direct for the Billet Scaur, still submerged by the tide, and we could not have been more than fifty yards from its end when he swung out again, with Marney still shooting.

Henry laughed then:

'If that cod of yours had any mates, we've given 'em a chance. That's as near the Billet Scaur as we dare shoot on an ebb tide.'

He had judged it well. We hadn't gone another hundred yards before Marney threw the last hook over, following it with another grapple and a marking buoy. The shooting was done, John opened the throttle. The coble swung round, and we were on our way back to the first buoy at full speed. There was no warmth in the sun. I was stiff and aching with the cold, but as excited as I had ever been fishing with rod and line when in less than twenty minutes we drew up to the buoy which Marney had flung over before the first real glimmer of day.

I was not such a fool as to expect to see a fish on every hook or even on a dozen. Mussels were soft, vulnerable. They could be eaten by crabs, before any fish discovered them. It did not follow that a fish actually seizing a bait would be hooked, or if hooked stay hooked for the duration of the time before it was hauled. Besides, the area of the sea's bed is boundless. Any fish could be in a thousand places, other than in the one where a bait had chanced to fall.

He picked up the buoy, hauled in the warp, coiling it neatly, then the grapnel, which he unbent and stowed. The line itself was in his hands and he started to haul. The engine was running at half throttle. Henry was steering so that we moved with the line, but slightly obliquely to it, so that I could see the hooks dangling on their snoods as they emerged, one every fathom, from the turgid water almost as fast as when they had been shot. There was no talking now. All three men were concentrating on the job. Henry at the tiller. John at the engine, both watching the line as Marney hauled, laying the coils neatly on the skep.

At least a score of them came in bare. Then I saw a swirling in the water, just ahead of the emerging line, then the gleam of a fish's belly. It came alongside. Holding the line in his left hand, Marney bent over with the gaff, swung it over the gunwale, and without comment went on hauling. It was a codling, not more than four pounds. John unhooked it and threw it in a fish crib. A few more bare hooks and in came another slightly smaller.

After that there was a monotonous succession of bare hooks, and already we were nearly halfway to Stoupe Beck where we had come to the end of the first line. Two codling from more than a hundred hooks! On several occasions, fishing at the Landing post or at Mill Beck I had caught more than a score, not so big as these but sizeable marketable fish if I'd had the mind to sell them.

Could these men possibly be making a living out of this? I didn't know then what price they were getting for their fish. It would be more than the twopence a pound for cod ruling in my boyhood, when even salmon brought only a shilling. But in those days, bread was only twopence for a full-sized loaf, milk twopence halfpenny a pint, butter ninepence, eggs a halfpenny each and never more than a penny, Woodbines or Guinea Gold a penny for five. If they got sixpence a pound for their codling, those two boxes which they had sent to market yesterday, the second box containing my own fortunate contribution, would not bring more than forty shillings, to be shared among the three of them and reckoned against the cost of bait (the mussels had to be bought), of fuel for the engine, the capital outlay on gear, and this without reckoning the days of bad weather when they were not able to fish at all.

Yet they all seemed happy enough. Even John's occasional gloomy outbursts were, I was certain, 'put on' as a brake against the cheerfulness and over-optimism of his brother. I hadn't seen the Fosdycks' catch yesterday. I guessed they had done no better, and probably not so well as the Lunns. They were not a happy-looking family, they never had been, yet they seemed to take things philosophically. Their coble was just in sight now, half a mile north of the Landing posts, two of them at the oars, one standing up, hauling.

But I still had my eyes on the line. The sun was mounting. There was perceptible warmth in it. I was cold, but no colder than I had been, and I was still hopeful that soon our fortunes would change. We were coming to Stoupe sands of happy memory.

Surely in that place that had once swarmed with fish, there would be something left alive. The first skep was now nearly full. There could only be a few hooks before the end of the line, and the start of the one that had been shot in a wide half circle over the sand itself. He hadn't reached it however when Marney shouted:

'There's summat coming now, either a big 'un or more than one.'

'And about time, too,' John muttered.

Again I saw that swirl on the water, the gleam of a fish. It was a small codling, and Marney heaved it on board without using the gaff. There were two more bare hooks. Then another, the biggest yet, a six pounder, with another on the next hook, and with it came the end of the line. John put the engine into neutral. While he unhooked the two fish, Marney quickly unbent the line, replaced the skep with an empty one and went on hauling. Henry reached forward and put the engine ahead again. There came another small codling, then more bare hooks.

We were steering shorewards now, over the sand. The hooks continued to come up bare. We moved in until we were not more than a hundred yards from the beach, where the Captain and I had landed to have our meal while we waited for the sile to come in. We turned seawards again and we were approaching the end of the sands and the start of High Batts scaurs, when Marney shouted:

'Here's another coming. Middling big.'

Would it be a plaice or dab or sole? We were still over sand. I saw it splashing, then a brown shape, turning white as it struggled belly up. But not till it came alongside did I see what it was, not a plaice or dab, but a skate, and a fairly big one about two feet across its kite-shaped body. As it came aboard with the gaff it gave a queer sort of gasping sound, almost a bark.

'That's no good to us,' Marney said, as he went on hauling. 'It might bring a bob on the market, with only its wings any good to eat and the rest only fit for pot bait. You'd better have it if you like skate' (this to me). 'You've got to hang skate wings for a few days though before you cook' em, else they taste of ammonia. . . Here's another fish.'

We must have been over the scaurs again. There was another small codling, and several more in rapid succession with one four pounder. The sand had failed yet it began to look as though we were going to do at least as well as they had done yesterday without my big cod. Was there a chance of another on that last line shot within yards of where I had caught it? Obviously it was that fish that had decided Henry on his course, when although avoiding the Fosdycks he might have chosen any other part of the Bay. The next line yielded only a couple of fish. We did better on the fourth and fifth, with one more six pounder, and several round about three pounds. And with the sixth line we started well, a fish big enough to be called a cod that must have weighed at least eight pounds, the biggest yet but still only half the size of my monster.

It was followed by a long blank in which some of the hooks came in, not bare, but with the bait still on them untouched. We were drawing shorewards again, getting nearer to the Billet Scaur. It was still awash, with only the shale, on to which I had hauled my fish, dry. We got nearer, still with no fish, and then just as we turned seawards again, as near to the scaur end as Henry had dared to steer when the line had been shot, Marney shouted:

'Eh—here's a big 'un coming. Bigger than yours,

I bet. I can hardly hold it. My, it's a big 'un.'

I was looking at the line, waiting for the splash, the slight sign of another monster. If I had looked at Marney instead I might have guessed by the smile on his face that he was joking. There *was* a fish. It was a small codling and it might have been the very one that I had first caught and thrown back. He held it up, dangling from the hook. I had to laugh. I'd been completely taken in. Henry was grinning, and even John had a half grin on his face when he growled:

'You bloody fool! I suppose you think that's funny! It's time you chucked fishing and got on the wireless as a comedian. You're enough to make a donkey laugh. But it would have surprised me if we had got a big 'un, here or anywhere else.'

'It would have done me really,' Henry said. 'But often where there's one there's more, and we haven't done so bad, as good as yesterday anyway.'

Marney was still hauling in the now fishless line nearing the end buoy. He was no longer smiling, and he made a significant remark which I guessed was made for my hearing.

'You know it's a mug's game this. But for lobstering there's nowt in it, and lobstering's no good in winter except in deep water with a bigger boat like the ones they've got at Whitby, where there's a harbour, and you can fish in almost any sort of weather. No need to launch up when you've done fishing. They've got a wheel-house for the skipper and a cabin with bunks, so you can stay out all night if you want and fish twice as many lines, and carry as many as four hundred lobster-pots when you're shifting grounds, not to mention herring nets. You ought to see our coble when we've got only one fleet of pots aboard, stacked up like a bloody furniture van. If I had the brass—'

'Well you haven't,' his father cut in sharply, 'so you can hold your jaw about going in for another boat.'

'Here—here!' said John. 'We've been into it all before.'

The remaining hooks came in all with their baits untouched. Marney in silence, hauled in the buoy. John opened the throttle. Henry swung the tiller round. There was enough sensation left in my fingers, which unlike theirs were dry, for me to search for and find in one of my inner pockets a packet of cigarettes, and hand it to Marney before he could find his own.

We were homeward bound.

19

DESPITE its physical discomforts and our disappointing catch I had enjoyed that first fishing expedition with the Lunns. If it had not reawakened my boyhood ambition to become a professional fisherman it had given me a salutary insight into someone else's problems for a change, problems which became more apparent as I got to know the family better.

Townspeople, taking their summer holidays by the sea, are apt to regard fishermen as a race of poor simple men who follow their hard dangerous calling because they are born and bred to it and lack the brains and imagination and ambition to think of anything better. They are admired for their picturesque appearance, especially the old white-bearded weather-beaten 'salts' sitting on empty fishboxes, mending nets or lobsterpots, splendid subjects for the camera.

This admiration may be of a different quality when the townsman at breakfast, or on his way to business in a steam-heated train in winter time opens his newspaper and reads of some heroic rescue performed by a lifeboat crew, or—making the headlines—of disaster in the course of a mission, the boat capsizing, the men thrown out, washed ashore dead, yet with another crew ready to take their place as soon as another lifeboat is available.

Their bravery is admired, but it is taken for granted, like that of soldiers, or sailors, or airmen in battle, of firemen or of rescue squads in coal-mine disasters. But what is not realised by those whose acquaintance with fishermen is confined to what they learn on summer holidays is that these men *have* brains, imagination and ambition. That fundamentally the problems they have to face are the problems that all families except the idle rich have to face whether they be fishermen, farmers, bus drivers, doctors, shopkeepers, clergymen and even poets and authors. They are the problems of employment, of money earning, of where to live and what to live in, and above all the attainment of a reasonable degree of happiness.

The Lunns were such a family, and what impressed me most about them was their vitality, their zest for living. Their problems were serious, but how serious I had not as yet realised. They were happy, too involved in physical activities for defeatist mental introspection, which is not to say that they were content with things as they were. I knew nothing about their financial situation. Obviously they were not impoverished. Whenever I chanced to enter the family living-room (and Mrs. Lunn kept 'open door') there were always signs of an abundance of food, either on the table or in smells coming from the oven. If there happened to be a meal on the way Mrs. Lunn would never fail to offer me a cup of tea or a tart or a cheese cake from the table. The young children were always well clad, with good footwear. Yet it was just as obvious that the men, at present at least, were working at a loss.

Mrs. Lunn's life was one of restless activity. She would be up before daybreak 'skaning' mussels for the lines, and even helping to bait them; cooking breakfast for her husband and John—still a bachelor and living at home. Then there would be the family breakfast to cook, the younger children to be got off to school, the washing up, the house to clean and the beds to make, dinner to be cooked for the children and the menfolk coming home, more washing up—not to mention a real washing on Mondays—and then helping to clean and bait the lines before another meal.

She was short, slender, a lovely woman to look at, a smile always flickering on her lips if she was not laughing. She was never still. If she sat down it would be to take up some mending, or a guernsey she was knitting either for her husband or John.

The two eldest daughters had already left home, one to be a children's nurse and help with a London family, the other a dressmaker in Leeds. Sally, the youngest, had a job in Whitby, which meant catching the early morning train and not getting home until the evening. She had inherited her mother's good looks, her skill at knitting and needlework, but if she was a willing helper in the family chores when she was home, it was not without signs of a subtle jealousy on her mother's part. Two birds had left the nest, as was right once they had learnt to fly. Sally was still a fledgling, but stretching her wings, feeling her independence, and with her own way of doing things, cooking the whole Sunday dinner for example, while mother took it easy. Mother wouldn't stand for that!

Marney, too, had left the nest. His wife was the daughter of the railway signalman, not a native of Bramblewick but of Leeds, and thus with an urban background. They had married soon after the war while Marney was still sailing as bo'sun on a tramp steamer and earning good money. Now they had a lively six-months-old daughter, and were living in a small cottage on the north cliff, one of the few that hadn't been snapped up by the townsfolk for summer holidays.

They were well matched. She was two years younger than Marney, pretty, with wavy brown hair, hazel eyes with long lashes, full lips and perfect teeth, a smooth clear complexion, a slender well-shaped figure. I guessed that she must have some difficulties in adapting herself to the special duties and anxieties of a fisherman's wife. But she was devoted to her husband and to their lovely baby, proud of them both, as he was of them.

She had mastered the difficult art of skaning mussels, inserting a knife between the two shells, giving it a twist right and left to cut the two adhering ligaments, then throwing the carcass into a pail of water to swell, although Mrs. Lunn could do it twice as fast. She had also learnt from Mrs. Lunn the complicated diamond and cable pattern of the traditional fisherman's guernsey, although her knitting and sewing was largely confined to the making of smaller garments for her first-born. Like Mrs. Lunn, too, she kept open house, but naturally I was averse to accepting anything substantial in the way of hospitality, as they, I knew instinctively, would be offended if I dared to make them, say, a gift of a packet of tea.

The truth was that these people were weaving a sort of spell over me. A spell more powerful than the place itself. I was being drawn irresistibly into their lives. Instead of moping over my own troubles, or indulging in the therapy of solitary angling, I had an urge to share in theirs, to be of practical help.

I had no inclination to go to sea with them just then, I did not funk the cold, but I had been a passenger, with no contribution to make in the way of helping with boat or gear. I made a point, however, of rising before daybreak to give at least a token assistance with the launching of both cobles, of being on the beach when they came in, of giving a shoulder at the capstan.

In any case there would not have been many opportunities for another trip. Following another week of clear frosty weather and calm sea during which both boats made only average catches there came one night a south-easterly gale of exceptional severity. It was accompanied by torrential rain. All the snow was gone by morning. The body of the sea where it was visible among the spume of the breaking waves was stained brown with the clay washed down from the cliffs and the swollen becks. It was an end for the time being not only to the coblemen's fishing, but to my own.

This did not mean a break in the family's activities. I found them, early in the afternoon, in a shed at the back of Henry's cottage busy with their lobster-pots, a stack of which were piled outside. It was still raining hard, with the sea roaring, the gale howling over the cottage roofs, but here we were in the lee of the south cliff, out of sight of the sea. The door of the shed was open. Just inside it John was bent down over a wooden frame which I recognised as the bottom of a lobsterpot. He was making holes in it at its corners with a red-hot poker, the pungent smoke drifting outside.

I stepped past him out of the rain. Henry and Marney, seated on empty fishboxes, each had the frame of a pot leaning against their knees and were braiding them with tarred cord, unwound from wooden needles.

Marney looked up from his task and said ironically: 'Eh—I thought you'd have been fishing, a nice day like this!'

John, the poker in his hand, had moved to a coal-stove at the far end of the shed. He thrust the poker into the glowing grate. He turned and said:

'What do you make of it, eh? Six days of fine weather, and then another bloody gale.'

Marney laughed:

'Listen to him. "Six days shalt thou labour and do all thy work, but the seventh day—" '

'I know—"is the Sabbath"—' John cut in, mockingly. ' "In it thou shalt not do any work, thou, nor thy son, nor thy daughter, thy manservant, nor thy cattle nor thy stranger that is within thy gate." You're not the only one who's been to Sunday School.'

'You two are wasting your time,' Henry said quietly. 'You ought to be local preachers. This isn't chapel. And it isn't a Sunday anyway. Don't you make them holes over big, John, or the hezel ends won't fit tight,' and to me, 'Eh—sit yoursen down by the fire, there's another box over there. Tak no notice of these lads of mine. They're always at each other. But they mean well. It's a beggar the weather coming on like this, but it gives us a chance to get on with our pots. We lost nearly all of 'em afore we started lining, in the back end. A gale like this came on sudden when we had 'em shot close in, and we hadn't time to shift 'em out to deep water.'

John was moving back with the red-hot poker.

'Them we didn't lose took almost as long to mend as making a brand new pot,' he said. 'We lost more than fifty quid's worth of gear, reckoning the tows. Fosdycks didn't lose any. They'd got their pots ashore.'

'And the Whitby chaps didn't either,' put in Marney. 'They'd got their pots miles out. That's where they score with their big craft, grounds we can't fish in our coble.'

'Now don't start that again,' said Henry. 'We'd done very well with lobsters up till then. Fishing's always an up-and-down job. It always was and it always will be.'

Marney took this rebuke in silence. Then he said:

'Well, there's one thing in favour of this gale blowing south-east. There'll be some wood washing up along Low Batts cliff. We've only got enough for one more pot. I'm going to have a walk along there soon as the tide ebbs.' And to me, 'We've got more than a hundred to make afore we start lobstering. If ever you happen to come across any likely looking planks on the beach, and you don't want them for kindling, save 'em for us. So long as they're not over thin or over thick. Three-quarter inch is the best, like that one John's making holes in.'

I had sat down and was watching Marney as he worked at his pot, the net growing rapidly from his nimble fingers, each mesh identical. Although since my boyhood lobster-pots had been one of the most familiar sights in the village in winter time, stacked up behind the cottages or sheds, I had never taken much interest in them. I had caught plenty of crabs and often lobsters in a more direct and interesting fashion. When the warm weather came, at low water of a spring tide, both were found in the deep cave-like crevices under the scaurs. To get them you had a long iron rod, with a crook at its end. You pushed this into the crevice, and you could tell by the sound of the rod grating on the shell if there was a crab or lobster there. Usually it would be too far in to see it. If you were lucky you would wriggle the crook end about until either it was seized by a claw, or you got it round its legs, then bit by bit you hauled it out. Lobsters as a rule were found in crevices which still contained water. You'd know it was a lobster when you heard the flapping of its tail. The first sign that it was coming out within reach of your fingers was the sight of the tip of its long red feelers, and you'd have to watch out for its claws.

I saw that the pot Marney was braiding consisted of a wooden-slatted base, with three hazel wands bent bow shaped, with their ends fixed in the base, one on each end, one in the middle. There was a straight wand securing these along the top and one at each side like the eaves of a house. He had covered one end with netting and was working along the top of the other end, forming a sort of netted roof.

Close by him was a finished pot. This had half of each side netted, but from the other halves netted funnels reached in to the middle. Through these funnels, attracted by the bait, the crabs or lobsters would enter. How these funnels were made I had at present no idea. What interested me was the base; the bows, the framework of the pot. I was confident that I could make one myself, for I had some skill at joinery. The one subject in which I had earned full marks at the secondary school I had attended was wood- and metalwork.

Diffidently I suggested that I should have a try.

'Aye, of course,' Henry said. 'We can do with a bit of help.' He pointed with his needle to a stack of driftwood in one corner of the shed. 'There's one board there will do when its sawn. Saw's a bit blunt. I meant to get it sharpened. Find him the hammer and nails, John.'

The saw *was* blunt. The board I tried it on was oak or teak, hard as iron, full of knots. But in the washhouse of my furnished cottage, which had once belonged to a ship's carpenter, was a chest of tools which included both a cross-cut and a rip-saw. There was also a small bench with a vice.

I hurried across, returning with both saws, which although rusty were sharp. I set to work, conscious that three pairs of eyes were watching me critically. I took my measurements from the base pieces that John had now finished burning the holes in. I cut five pieces, two a couple of feet in length for the sides, three shorter ones for the ends and middle. I got my first objection from Marney when I spaced them out for nailing.

'You've got 'em the wrong way round. Short pieces have got to go on top of the long 'uns. And mind you've got to drive the nails so that you clench 'em inside, otherwise their points will lift with wear and tear and they'll get plenty of that. Otherwise he's shaping all right for a beginner, isn't he?'

'He's doing all right,' Henry said.

'It's putting in the bows that's tricky,' said John.

I was aware while I started the nailing that John was preparing for this very operation. There were a number of hazel wands hanging on a peg on the wall. They were already partly bent U-shape with pieces of twine. He took one, removed the twine, and with a knife slightly sharpened the ends. He inserted one end into one of the holes he had burned with the poker, and twisted it round until it was firm. Then he coaxed the other end into the opposite hole, and pushed hard, maintaining a pressure on the top of the bow so as to keep its shape. He had to borrow the hammer then to drive a nail through the ends of the base, and the ends of the bow to secure them permanently.

I carried on with the hammer while he prepared another bow. Mine so far was a simple enough job, and in spite of intermittent hammer borrowing I soon had the first part of it nailed together, ready for the slats, which had to be measured and sawn. I was enjoying myself anyway, highly pleased with the thought I might be really helping my friends instead of just watching. I'd be more help still if I could learn to make a complete pot, doing the braiding too; and even more exciting if when they started fishing, I could see one of my own making hauled in with crabs or lobsters in it.

Fortunately there was a duplicate poker. I successfully made the six holes in my completed base. But in bending the first bow I put too much pressure on it and it cracked.

'Don't worry about that,' Marney said, encouragingly. 'Chuck it away and try another. We've got plenty of hezels, although we'll want a lot more afore we've finished the job.'

I got the next one in all right, although it looked a bit lop-sided. After I had fixed the other two, John moved over and deftly adjusted them, so that they were all of equal height and shape. The fixing of the three straight sticks, one at the top, one at each side, was simple. Apart from that slight help I'd done it all myself, and I felt like shouting 'cock-a-doodle-do'.

Marney said:

'You've made a good job of it. We'll make a fisherman of you yet. Do you know how to braid?'

'No,' I said, 'but I'm willing to learn.'

All this time he and Henry had never stopped work on their own pots. Marney had finished covering the two ends and top. He was now forming a number of loops round one of the four vacant spaces left along the sides.

'There's nowt in it,' he said. 'Any bairn could do it, only it wants a bit of practice making the spouts.

I'm on with a spout now. You've got to decrease your meshes, making the spout smaller as you go on. Just watch me.'

If Mrs. Lunn had been trying to teach me how to knit one of her guernseys I could not have been more bewildered. By spout it was clear that he meant the braided funnels through which the crab or lobster entered the pot. But all I could see was a confusion of loose meshes growing outwards from the loops he had first made. In a few minutes, however, this was about eight inches in length and I saw that the number of meshes had been reduced by at least half, that the row he was working on were half meshes instead of complete diamond, so that they formed one continuous line. When he had made the last one, he pushed the whole lot inside the pot, stretched it to the opposite side-stick and made it fast with the twine from his needle. He cut the twine, and tied a piece to the small end of the spout and made this fast to the side-stick. There was no confusion now, but a perfectly shaped funnel leading halfway into the pot, and although I had watched closely, I still hadn't grasped how he had done it. I must have shown this by a mixed look of admiration and bewilderment on my face, for he laughed:

'That's all there is to it. You'll soon learn if you want to. But you'll not want to mucky your hands with tarry twine. I've got a ball of clean twine at home, and we can tak your frame over and braid it there tonight in front of our kitchen fire nice and comfortable. I'm off to the beach now afore anyone else picks up the wood. Is anyone else coming?'

'I'm not,' said John. 'Thank you very much, I'm going to get this pot braided.'

'We'll come down and give you a hand if there's

more than a load,' said Henry.

I didn't hesitate to answer 'yes', for I rarely failed to take a walk along the beach when the tide had ebbed low enough in stormy weather. To do this had been one of boyhood's biggest thrills, especially if there were no footprints on the sand to show that someone had been there before me, for all sorts of treasures would be left on the beach at high-water mark, apart from driftwood, and if you scraped among the sand and shingle, often coins and other valuables.

Now with Marney I was aware of a new interest. I was obsessed with this ambition to make a complete lobster-pot. If Marney could teach me to do the braiding with 'clean' twine, I was not going to jib at 'muckying' my hands with the pleasant-smelling tarry stuff, once I had acquired some of his proficiency. If I could make one I could make more. If I only made half a dozen in time for when they started fishing, I'd have the satisfaction of knowing that I'd done something to help, something better than adding one big fish to their meagre hard-won catch. And there would be the thrill of seeing them hauled with lobsters in them.

It had stopped raining, but the wind was violent as ever, and we felt the full fury of it as we walked down the slipway to the beach. In gusts it was blowing almost with hurricane force. Rarely had I seen the sea so rough. The whole Bay was a mass of broken water. Gigantic waves were rolling in on the Landing Scaurs. The noise was like continuous thunder. We paused. Marney was staring seawards.

'That's a queer thing,' he said. 'I can't see the low posts. Dammit. They've gone. They've washed away. It's like a chap whose lost his two front teeth. They were there this morning.'

The gale was blowing full in my face, my eyes filling with tears, and it was with difficulty that I was able to confirm Marney's observation. Where before there had been five posts, three on the East Scaur, two on the West, there were now only three. The two outer ones which marked the vital mouth had gone. And the one left on the West Scaur—they were all like the one I had used to lean my rod against, thick oak saplings—was bending and shaking as the waves crashed by it.

'That means another job for us and the Fosdycks,' Marney muttered. 'If them posts haven't washed up, we'll have to get new 'uns, and dig fresh holes for them in the scaur. Not that there's likely to be any use for them if this weather goes on. I tell you I'm fed up with the whole carry on.'

I suspected that Marney had something on his mind, quite apart from the weather and the missing posts. He was silent as we walked along under the north cliff, buffeted by the wind, dodging the thick masses of spume driving up from the scaurs. We passed the Gunny Hole Nab, where I had not fished since my alarming experience. Beyond it there was a little shingly beach, after which the cliffs rose higher and more abruptly and formed another bluff which left only a few yards between its base and the nearest margin of the sea, although this, as it had done at the Billet Scaur, was surging in and out in accordance with the breaking and back-wash of the waves.

The bluff, in any weather on a flood tide, but especially on a spring one, was a deceptive bottle neck for anyone venturing along the shore of Low Batts cliff. Many a time in summer, visitors had been trapped by it, and the pleasure boatmen, always keeping a sharp look out, would make an extra shilling or two going to their rescue, although there were plenty of places where they would be safe until the tide ebbed again.

Beyond the bluff the cliff rose higher, but still nothing like that of High Batts. The shore receded and here, for its entire length to the actual point, it consisted of huge slabs of rock which, in the course of time, had fallen from the cliff, where, alternating with soft shale, were thick beds of ironstone hard almost as granite.

The slabs were piled up in confusion, some flat, some on edge or leaning on other smaller ones, and the spaces between them were filled with spume and drifted weed. We had to jump from one slab to the next so that our progress was slow. We hadn't got far when we sighted one of the posts, close to the cliff bottom and just short of what would have been high-water mark. I recognised it by the notch as the very one I had used for my rod on the West Scaur. It had broken off just an inch or two below, where it was at least a foot thick, the splinted fracture reaching down to where it had been cemented into the scaur.

Marney gave the post a kick with his deck-booted foot, as though it symbolised for him an enemy.

'By gum,' he said. 'That shows you what the sea can do, snapping off an oak post as thick as that like a carrot. It's not surprising that our pots get smashed up in seas not half so bad as this, no matter how well you make them.' He gave the post another kick. 'Do you know I get fed up with this game at times,' he went on. You spend hours and days, aye even months making pots, only to see 'em smashed up, sooner or later. And dammit, lobsters are the only things that do pay these days. Some of those Whitby boats make anything up to a hundred quid a week from when they start lobstering, and some of them are doing it the whole year round. They work as many as four hundred pots and fish deepwater grounds that no one thought had lobsters on them a few years ago. That's what we ought to be doing instead of messing on as we have been. Father's as good a fisherman as any of those, better than most. Although he wasn't potting during the war—he hadn't time to make any pots—he did well—lining and trawling and drifting for herring and mackerel in that motor mule fishing out of Whitby, although he only took a skipper's share from the owner. The owner offered to sell it to him for eight hundred quid when the war was over. Mind, it wasn't as good as one of those big craft fishing out of Whitby now, but it would have been a damn sight better than staying on here.'

I was surprised by Marney's outburst. I said:

'Eight hundred pounds is a lot of money.'

He laughed.

'Those big craft cost twice as much! But the chaps who have 'em don't put all the brass down. It's like buying a house or owt else that's expensive. So much down and the rest paid back in instalments, with interest of course, and maybe for years before it's all paid off. But what does that matter if you're making a living and you get it in the end?'

'Then why didn't he buy it? He must have saved a bit of money if he'd been doing so well?'

Marney hesitated, then he said thoughtfully:

'I don't know. I don't know. And mind don't let on to him or anyone else what I'm telling you, or he'd bite my head off. But I have an idea that it's all because of mother. I have an idea that he must have talked it over with her, but that she was dead against buying anything that couldn't be paid for in cash. She'd rather starve than go into debt would mother. Besides, she hadn't liked him fishing from Whitby during the war, with him often spending nights at sea, and me and John being away too. She was set on having us all back home when the war was over. If we did get a big boat it wouldn't mean just fishing from Whitby. It would mean we'd all have to go and live there and that's just what we'll have to do when the Fosdycks pack up as they're bound to do, with Luke and Tindal getting on for seventy. Even with lobsters, fishing at Bramblewick's played out. It's either that or giving up fishing altogether. . . Come on let's shift this post above high-water mark. We'll have to wait for calm weather before we can come for it in the coble and tow it back and rig it up again. Mind not a word about what I've been telling.'

The post was too heavy to lift direct. We had to drag it one end at a time until it was well above the last high-tide mark. The rain still held off, but the gale was as fierce as ever, with the spume from the breakers flying through the air like clotted soap suds. Marney was silent again as we carried on along the cliff foot and over the slabs of rock. There was no sign of the second post. We found a few pieces of drift-wood but only one board of suitable dimensions. We had almost reached the point when we saw ahead of us a conspicuous object among the rocks. As we drew near we saw that it was a fishbox, and that within a few yards, and still awash in the run of the waves, there were two more. Marney cheered up as he examined the first. It was empty, of course, and without a lid, the type used on board trawlers for off-loading fish onto the quay side, strongly made. Burnt on to it on each side was the name of a Dutch fishing port.

'This is a bit of luck,' he said. 'There's enough here for two pot bottoms, and that makes six with those other two. It's an ill wind that blows nobody good. They must have washed off the deck of a Dutchman, and if he was fishing inside the three-mile limit sarve him bloody well right. We'll walk on and see if there's any more before turning back. We might find that other post too. But we'll have to look sharp. With the wind where it is tide will be turning fore it's gone full ebb, and we've got to get round the nab. Don't forget you're coming to our spot tonight to finish that pot. And mind not a word of what I've been telling to Amy. Women can never keep their mouths shut.'

20

IT was a morning in mid February. We were on our way in the coble for the first hauling of the pots. They had been shot, a hundred and twenty of them, in three 'fleets' of forty each, more than a mile out in deep water on muddy ground, where, according to my friends there were no lobsters, but a chance of a fair haul of crabs, although it was too early in the year to expect a crib full, the crib being the long deep container under the mid-ship thwart in which the codling on that, to me, memorable occasion in cold December had made such a poor showing.

The reason for shooting the pots in deep water was that they were dry, and in spite of the pieces of iron or stones lashed inside to their bottoms, semi-buoyant. It would take several days of immersion before the air in the cells of the wood was forced out by the pressure of the sea, and the wood became waterlogged, making the pots more resistant to drifting. Besides, as Marney had explained to me in the course of my 'education', lobsters were fastidious creatures. A new pot had to be seasoned before it was much use for them. They didn't like the smell of tar. In fact it would be better not to use tarred twine for the braiding if it wasn't that it lasted longer. We'd prove that when we saw how the pot whose bottom I had made myself (and in the braiding of which he had given me my first lesson) fished. He'd be willing to bet that it would catch two lobsters to the other's one, until they'd got seasoned.

I was still a passenger, an onlooker. But yesterday I had helped to carry the pots down to the coble, aground on the slipway foot, before the tide came in, and stack them on board, not the whole lot for with one fleet, with its coils of rope, buoys and anchors there was scarcely room to move. I had stayed ashore when as soon as the tide was in, they had pushed off, and it was not until they had returned from shooting the second fleet, and had loaded the third, that I finally joined them, and then it was with a special interest. In that fleet, was not only the one on which Marney had given me my lesson, but five more braided with tarred twine, 'all my own make', and alas easily recognisable as such, particularly by the shape of the spouts.

I had been a very willing but a far from adept pupil. The knot used in braiding has a deceptive simplicity. The 'needle' is a thin piece of tough wood or bone (superseded now by plastic) an inch wide for the size of mesh used for a lobster-pot with one bluntly pointed end, and the other with a U-shaped groove. Short of the pointed end is a cavity with a pointed flexible prong. The twine is coiled over this prong by way of the groove, until the needle is 'full'. As it is used it is automatically paid out.

With plain braiding, you start with a rod, or in the case of a pot a length of twine stretched tight between the two ends of the first bow, close to the base. On this you form loops, spaced the width of a mesh apart and half a mesh in length, working from left to right. When you have formed the last loop, the twine goes round the bow, and back into the last loop. You draw it until it forms the shape of a complete mesh, grip the loop with a finger, push the needle over and across and down, draw it tight and your knot is made. You go on until you reach the first loop, then you work backwards, and each knot now gives you a completed mesh, with the same number of half-formed meshes left.

But Marney's meshes were all identical in size. Mine were not. One row would be small, so that I could hardly get the needle into the free loops. The next would be correspondingly big, and instead of producing diamonds my meshes were all shapes and sizes. Yet none was big enough, I hoped, to permit the escape of a full-sized lobster or crab, and it was only with the spouts of the pots I had made entirely on my own that he had been really critical. In shaping them the trick was to take in two loops instead of one for some of the rows of meshes, so that gradually the length was reduced, but which loops and how many beat me. His spouts and Henry's and John's were all alike. Mine all varied in shape and size. Some of them I had cut out in exasperation and braided them over again, with no better result. But as Marney had said, the proof would be whether they fished well or not. If they didn't he could easily put new ones in himself.

The weather yesterday had been propitious, with only a light offshore wind and the sea calm. There had indeed been a subtle touch of spring in the mild land scented air which seemed to infect my three companions. They had been unusually cheerful, and even the Fosdycks had been less grumpy as they had helped us down with the coble. They had given up their winter long lining, but they wouldn't start potting until March, this being their unvarying custom.

All six of my pots had been the first of that last fleet to be shot after the buoy, and the long warp and anchor had gone over. Each pot was tied to the main rope, called the tow, by a two-fathom length of slightly lighter rope, and there was a distance of four fathoms between each pot. The baits were chunks of codling that had been kept from the last long-lining trip earlier in the week, with some 'heads' and carcasses of filleted fish from the local fishmonger. But I had been able to make a contribution with a few small codling I had caught at my favourite spot down the Landing where the post had been cemented in again, with a coble mast making a temporary replacement of the other post at the end of the opposite East Scaur.

As Marney had thrown the pot with the untarred braiding over he had shouted:

'What's the betting on that pot having a lobster in it when we come to haul?'

'Don't talk so daft,' said John. 'There's no lobsters out here.'

'I have known it happen,' Henry said. 'But not often. Lobsters, like any other shell-fish, wander about, and it stands to reason they're on soft ground sometimes.'

I had observed that Marney had baited that pot with the biggest of my own codling, which might have made two baits if it had been cut. I said, jokingly:

'I'll take you on. A packet of Woodbines if it comes up empty!'

It was another lovely day with the wind still light and offshore and a scarcely perceptible swell. There was only a thin scattering of clouds high in the sky. There was a real warmth in the sunshine. Fishing in conditions like this was indeed a pleasant occupation, and I was sure as we drew near to the buoy of the first fleet that Marney was not at present thinking about his un-attainable dream boat and other problems. That he was excited as I was myself. He was already putting on his oilskin apron.

It was, however, the first fleet we were approaching, not the one with my own pots, and when having picked up the buoy he let it go again, and just hauled on the corked warp to which it was attached, I saw that this was going to be a different sort of job from hauling in lines. John had stopped the engine. He too had put on an oilskin apron, and he took hold of the warp to give Marney a hand. I moved to join him but I was waved aside by Henry.

'We can manage,' he said. 'It's when we're hauling pots in bad weather against the tide that we sometimes could do with an extra hand.'

'Aye,' said John. 'Especially with new tarred tows, stuck with sand and cutting your hands to bits.'

'This is a picnic,' Marney said. 'Here's the anchor.'

He gave the warp, which had been slanting at first with the tide and had now become vertical, an extra heave. He hauled in faster, with John paying the slack overboard. Up came the anchor, and this too went overboard as Marney seized the tow, hauled in a short length bent over the side, lifted in the first pot, and set it down on the lid of the engine box.

It was to me an incredible sight. For there in it were at least a score of crabs, all of them well above the legal size of four and a half inches across the broadest part of their shells. Some were on the bottom of the pot, on top of each other, some clinging to the braided ends and sides. One very big one was actually jammed in the narrow end of one of the spouts. Only the bones of a codling's head were left on the bait string in the middle of the pot. There could scarcely have been room for another.

I expressed my astonishment.

'Does it often happen like this?'

'I wish it did,' Henry laughed. 'And with every pot. But it's a good spot this at this time of the year. They're nice crabs too.'

'You wait till we haul that white pot of yours,' shouted Marney. 'It won't be crabs, it'll be lobsters.'

He was holding on to the tow. There were two doors to the pot, one on each side, diagonally with the spouts. Henry and John had opened them, and were rapidly pulling out the crabs and throwing them into the crib. When it was empty, John cleared the bones of the cod head from the bait string, replaced it with another piece of fish, fastened the door and heaved the pot over. They went on hauling, the coble moving astern as he did so for the tow was now functioning like the cable of an anchor. In came another pot, again crammed with crabs.

I said:

'This looks a better proposition than lining. How much are crabs worth these days.'

'I'll tell you what,' said John, as he pulled a fair-sized one out and held it up, 'If you wanted to buy one like this in a fishmonger's shop say in Leeds, boiled of course, I bet you'd have to pay at least four bob for it.'

'Well they ought to fetch twelve bob a stone on Whitby market,' Marney put in. 'Them chaps who've been potting in their big boats right through the winter sometimes get as much as fifteen bob a stone, and as much as fifteen bob a piece for lobsters.'

'Aye,' said Henry. 'But how many do they catch to get that price?'

They were getting on thin ice again, and I interrupted quickly:

'How many crabs to a stone?'

'There'll be more than a stone in this pot, and t'other one we've hauled,' Marney said. 'But they won't all be as full as these. . .' And to his father and John he said, 'Look sharp getting 'em out. There's two more fleets to haul after this. God—you're slow.'

The pot was emptied, re-baited and thrown over. Another one came in. Again it was practically full. How different I thought this was from the long lining I had witnessed, the monotonous succession of bare hooks, between those with fish on them. If Marney was right about the market price of twelve shillings a stone then already from three pots there was more than thirty shillings worth in the crib. If they went on like this with the rest of the pots the total value wouldn't 'be far short of fifty pounds. If this was repeated every day for a week, then the total would be the fantastic one of three hundred pounds, probably considerably more than my friends had earned in the whole of the winter's lining.

And it did go on, pot after pot, all with one solitary exception packed with crabs. The exception came towards the end of the fleet, a pot containing not a single crab, but curled up inside it a large conger eel, which Marney hailed as a 'bit of luck'. When cut up it would make at least a dozen pot baits. John was not so happy about it. After several attempts to get it out with his hands, he had to use the gaff. It had left the inside of the pot and his hands, too, covered with slime. The slime was still on his hands when with the last pot of the fleet cleared of its catch, re-baited and shot he had to use the starting-handle.

'They're the muckiest bloody things that ever was are congers,' he growled. 'If you haul up any more, Marney, you can get 'em out yoursen.'

But he was grinning as the engine, with one

swing of the handle, started. Even John could not be indifferent to the fact that things were going very well.

We hadn't to move far to the second fleet. It seemed to me impossible that this phenomenal good fortune could continue, and indeed the first pot that was hauled in contained only two crabs. But the next was packed tight, and from then on not one had less than half a dozen, and there were no more congers. It was a slow but still exciting business. I was only wishing that I could have taken an active part in it. Would my own pots prove that they would work as well as these, in spite of their amateurish spouts? Would Marney's optimism about the untarred pot be justified? Would it contain a lobster?

The crib was nearly full when we came to the last pot of the second fleet. I had been watching the two buoys of the third fleet, with the nearest not more than a hundred yards away. As we steamed towards it Marney said:

'You're going to cough up that packet of Woodbines.' And then to my delight he added, 'Eh—would you like to haul it in once we've got the anchor on board?'

I was in my usual spectator's place in the bows and I eagerly moved over as Marney picked up the buoy.

'There won't be any lobster in it,' John said. 'He's only having you on.'

I hadn't much doubt that Marney was pulling my leg, but that made no difference to my excitement as, with the anchor up, Marney handed me the tow and I got the weight of it. The anchor went over. I hauled until I came to the short strop of the pot, and I saw the pot itself. It came in within reach of my hands. With Marney holding the tow I lifted it in over the gunwale on to the engine box. And Marney gave a shout.

'There you are! Didn't I tell you?'

I still thought he was pulling my leg. The pot was as full as any of the others with crabs. And it was not until he opened one of the doors and pulled out one of the crabs that I saw under it a lobster, not more than six inches in length. He took it out, held it up.

'Why,' said John. 'It's nowt a ninnycock.'

'Aye, but it's a lobster,' said Henry. 'I wouldn't really have believed it out here on mud among the crabs!'

'To tell you the honest truth I wouldn't either,' Marney confessed. 'It's a miracle.'

I slapped him on the shoulder.

'You win,' I said. 'And I'll make it another packet if there's a lobster in the next pot, "all my own make". But it's undersize, isn't it? Shouldn't it go back?'

The legal size of lobsters I knew was nine and a half inches from the beak to the tip of the tail. This was far short of that, but I could see that Marney was hesitating.

'It's up to you,' he said. 'There's no one likely to find out if you keep it hid when we get ashore. Shall I or shan't I?'

I was tempted too. But this pot, apart from the frame, was not my own make. The spouts, the most vital part of the apparatus were Marney's. I was more concerned with seeing what was in the next pot, whether my crudely made spouts had worked, if not with lobsters, at least with the swarming crabs.

'Let it go!' I said.

He dropped it overboard. I counted the remaining crabs as he and John took them out. There were eight, making ten altogether with the lobster. It was re-baited and shot. I went on hauling. The pot came in sight, and as I lifted it out I could tell by the sheer weight of it that I had not worked in vain. I set it down on the engine box. With its odd-shaped meshes and spouts, it certainly looked what it was, the product of an amateur. I had not expected a lobster, but it contained, and I counted them, nine crabs, and Henry said, as though reading my mind:

'It's a good pot. Every bit as good as one of ours, never mind how it looks. The main thing is that it does the job.'

There were only five crabs in the next pot, but the following three had so many I didn't bother to count them. And with only a few exceptions it was so with the rest of the pots in the fleet. Then, with the last pot emptied of its catch, re-baited and shot, the anchor and buoy flung over, John started the engine. We headed for home. My hands were wet and before I could get my packet of cigarettes from my pocket Marney was handing round his own. I saw him glance at the crib. It was not only packed full, there was an overflow into two big baskets. And he said, with what I thought was a gorgeous nonchalance:

'We haven't done so bad, have we?'

Henry was smiling.

'Better than I thought we would,' he said. 'I've only known crabs as thick as this once before and years ago, when you were lads and I was fishing with Jack and Gilbert Knaggs. Just after we'd come from Flamborough. But there were so many others at it then we only got three bob a stone for them.'

'Aye, we've done well,' was John's comment. 'But we'll be lucky if we do as well tomorrow.'

He said this with a grin, however.

I made no immediate comment. I was looking at the overflowing crib, immensely happy in the thought that for once the tide had turned for my friends and that my 'own' six pots had made at least a tiny contribution to their prodigious catch. But this had been a fine weather picnic where everything had gone right. It wouldn't often be like this. I wished that I could do more for them. It was true, as Marney had said, that fishing at Bramblewick was played out. A catch such as this would not compensate for the unprofitable months of winter fishing. When the Fosdycks retired it would be impossible for them to carry on. If only I was rich! If only I could myself buy for them this big fishing boat that Marney dreamed about and set them all on the way to the prosperity they deserved.

21

I WAS awakened long before daybreak next morning by a terrific clap of thunder. I jumped out of bed, drew back the curtains and was dazzled by a flash of lightning, followed almost instantly by another reverberating thunder clap, and then by the noise of wind and driving hailstones.

I hurriedly dressed, and with the light of a torch, for the village gas lamps were always put out by half past ten at night, made my way down to the Dock. It was winter again. The ground was white all over. The hailstones were driving in my face as I approached the slipway top. The wind, and it couldn't be far short of gale force, was blowing in from the roaring invisible sea, which yesterday had been so innocently calm in the spring-like sunshine.

I had spent the evening in Marney's cosy cottage. I had shared with him and his pretty wife a crab supper, and crabs when caught at the right time of the year, when they are full of meat and not watery, beat lobster. We'd had them dressed of course, with tea, and bread and butter, and finished up with cheese cakes, warm from the oven. Marney was washed, wearing his best guernsey with a white silk scarf knotted round his neck, slippers on his feet instead of seaboots. The meal over he had busied himself with a door-mat he was making out of unlaid manilla rope, knitting it in a similar fashion to ordinary knitting but using only his fingers. He was going to teach me how to do it as soon as he could get hold of another piece of untarred rope, tar in any shape or form being taboo in the living-room. Amy too, when she had washed up (she had refused my offer of help) had started work on a half-finished baby garment. The baby had been asleep in her cot in a darkened corner of the room until ten o'clock, when, at a word from Amy, Marney had tenderly picked her up and deposited her on her mother's lap for her ten o'clock feed.

They were indeed a happy family. It was a lovely child, rosy cheeked, healthy and contented. I guessed that Amy must have been feeling very pleased about the day's catch, and the prospect of further good fortune. Marney had listened with the headphones of his rather primitive radio to the night weather forecast. There had been no hint in it of any appreciable change, and when about half past ten I had taken my leave it was with the mutual understanding that we'd be going to sea again in the morning as soon as it was light.

What a hope! It was now round about four o'clock. It wouldn't be light before eight. I couldn't imagine that my friends had not been awakened by that double peal of thunder and the noise of the wind, but there was no sign of any of them coming down to the Dock. What could they have done anyway? Both cobles were safe. So presumably were the pots, anchored well out in the Bay away from the rocks. But unless there came another miraculous change in the weather, the chances of our going out to haul them, of another big catch of crabs were nil. This was a north-easter. The thunderclaps, the heavy downpour of hail were typical. There was one more flash of lightning but seconds passed before I heard the distant rumble of thunder over the land. The hail ceased, and there was a moment of relative calm before the wind came again, heralding another squall.

I walked down the slipway. The tide was flowing and had already reached its foot. I had to stop short of it as a huge wave swept in and broke, its run reaching almost to my feet. As far as I could see in the beam of my torch, there was nothing but curling wind-swept waves and broken water. There would be no fishing today. I made my way back to my cottage and to bed.

*

The gale lasted off and on for a week, a week in which, had the weather remained as it had been on the day of our first haul, and my calculations been correct, my friends might have been richer by the sum of at least three hundred pounds. There was one compensation, large quantities of drift-wood, mostly dunnage thrown overboard by passing ships, and consisting of rough planks washed up along the shores. There was raw material for the bottoms for at least one more fleet of pots. And whether they had a hunch of what was to come, or were simply incapable of inactivity, the family was busy again in the shed, and with a new confidence, born of seeing those pots of mine full of crabs, and with a little more skill with the braiding, I helped them.

The gale had not been so violent as the south-easter in December. There had been intervals of comparative calm but they had never lasted long enough for the heavy swell to die down and leave the Landing navigable. In such intervals with my field-glasses—like my greatcoat a souvenir of my Air Force days—we had been able to see all six buoys, heaving up and down in the swell, and Marney had remarked with disgust—we were alone on the cliff top:

'If we'd been fishing from Whitby instead of being stuck in this damned spot, we could be hauling them now. And think of the crabs that might be in them!'

The storm cone, with its point upwards, had been hauled on the coastguard's flagstaff the morning of the gale, telling us, as Marney remarked sarcastically, 'summat we already knew'. It had stayed there all week until the morning when, with the wind backed to the west and the swell still heavy but no longer breaking across the Landing mouth, we put to sea again.

I sensed from their tight-lipped silence that my friends were bothered. All three of them were staring ahead. Henry as usual at the tiller, John and Marney standing amidship, swaying with the movement of the coble as she rode the long rollers. Before we were halfway there the buoys were in sight, but only when they too rose with the waves. John was the first to speak, and it was with a more than customary gloomy voice.

'I can only see four buoys. One fleet must have gone adrift.'

'Then, it's time you got your eyesight tested,' Marney snapped. 'I can see six. There's three of them clumped together.'

'Then one fleet *must* have drifted. We're in for trouble all right!'

Henry said nothing, but his expression was grim.

As we drew near I could see how John had been mistaken in his count. Instead of the six buoys being spaced two to each fleet, and the length of their tow apart, three of them were almost touching each other. One fleet *had* drifted. The three other buoys were riding clear, and at a normal distance.

We approached the three buoys in silence. John stopped the engine. Marney picked up one of the buoys, hesitated for a moment, then slowly began to haul in the warp. As he did so the other two buoys began to move in towards the coble. Obviously their warps had fouled. Soon he had three warps in his hands, twisted together but still slack, for he hadn't got to the strain of the anchors. The two buoys came in. The twisted ropes began to tighten, to reach vertically down from the coble side. John took hold, then Henry, both straining now to lift not one anchor but three, and the weight of the pots that were nearest to them.

I was sadly aware of my own present impotence. There was no room on the warps for me to help. I could just watch, taking some comfort in the thought which I felt they must be sharing that in spite of this muddle produced by the gale, the pots were still here, and not as had happened so often in the past washed ashore and smashed on the rocks. And I was still hopeful that we were going to have some sort of a catch. Seeing that they had been in the water so long, it might even be as big as our first one!

Slowly the warps came in, still twisted together. They were not paid overboard however but coiled on top of the buoys in the stern. An anchor came in. This too was stowed. There came another anchor, making the end of two warps and the beginning of two tows. Then Marney bent down over the gunwale. He lifted in two pots, bound tightly together in a tangle of ropes that also contained the third anchor, its warp and the beginning of its tow. One of those pots I recognised. Its braiding, or what was left of it was untarred. It was the one that had caught the little lobster, and the crabs I had counted with such satisfaction. There were no crabs in it now. The braiding was torn. Two of the bows had caved in. Apart from the spouts and the bottom it was a wreck. The second pot, which was not one of my own and clearly belonged to one of the other fleets, was in similar condition.

Another wrecked pot came in. Then there was a halt in the hauling. The tows were made fast. All three men began sorting out the tangle of pots, strops and tows. It seemed to me that a family of kittens left alone in a wool shop could not have created a more confusing muddle. But shortly Marney lifted my own pot clear. He had untied it from the tow, and he said to me, laconically:

'Eh—tak it and stow it in the bow will you? Tight up as far as it'll go. There'll be a lot more to come.'

I was glad that at last I was going to be of some help. I stowed it. He handed me the second one with which it had been entangled. There was now some muttered conversation between all three which I could not follow. Then at last I heard Henry say:

'We're all clear now. Drop that anchor over and we'll get this fleet aboard and come back for t'other two. I doubt we're going to find the whole lot of 'em scrubbed. It would have been all right if they hadn't been new pots. Another week and they would all have been soaked. But it's no use crying over spilt milk.'

'I'm not crying over spilt milk,' growled John. 'Oh, dear, no! There's more than milk been spilt with this do.'

'If we'd been fishing out of Whitby we could have hauled 'em three days ago when the wind dropped,' Marney said. 'They hadn't drifted then. We could see the buoys all clear.'

Whether Henry had heard that remark or not he made no comment.

An anchor went over, followed by its warp and buoy. There were two tows left now. One was paid out, followed by the second anchor and tow, warp and buoy, and hauling was renewed on the third tow from which the last two pots had been detached.

The weather was still favourable. Apart from the swell the sea was calm, and the actual hauling presented no difficulties. I could have done it myself. Pot after pot came aboard in a process more discouraging than the bare hooks of the codlines. All were empty. There was not one that hadn't suffered some sort of damage, either to the frame or braiding. It was clear that owing to their semi-buoyancy they had swung about on the bottom during the storm, like balloons on a string. As they came in, they were detached from the tow, handed to me and stowed, with Marney shouting directions to me from time to time as to where to lay the next one. The stack was well above the height of the gunwales before half of the fleet was in.

And this was only the start of the day's work. All the pots, including those of the other two fleets would have to be carried up to the warehouse. Days, possibly weeks, would have to be spent repairing them, and in that time no matter how favourable the weather, there could be no fishing. What a gamble it was! One day a fortune in sight, then disaster. How I wished that it could be otherwise.

The last pot came in. Ironically, although there was a big gash in the braiding, it contained a single crab. Marney laughed as he pulled it out through the gash.

'Well one's better than nowt. We'll have to draw lots for who's to have this for tea.'

With the anchor and buoy in, he had to come to my assistance with the stowing of that pot, for the stack, now high above the gunwales, was swaying dangerously with the movement of the coble. John had started the engine. We turned shorewards, lit cigarettes. Because of the space taken up by the pots I had moved to the after part of the boat. We smoked in silence for a time, and it was Henry who at last spoke, slowly almost as though he was speaking his thoughts aloud:

'You know, it's a nuisance pots taking up so much room in a coble. I wish someone would invent a pot that would fold up flat when it wasn't in use, but that would open up like the lid of a box when you came to shoot it. It would be a boon and a blessing. It would be better still, if it would stand up to rough weather better than ours, and yet fish as good.'

'Well, I've seen plenty of pots shut up flat,' put in John, sarcastically. 'There's some of these not far off it.'

Marney said nothing. Neither did I. But those words of Henry's had started something in my mind. Something which was to affect dramatically the pattern of my life. It was the genesis of the Walmsley Patent Collapsible Indestructible Lobster-Pot.

22

FOR the next year that patent lobster-pot dominated my mind and all my activities, to the exclusion even of my private angling. I saw in it not only a solution to one of my friends' biggest problems, this recurrent loss and damage to gear, but ultimate prosperity for them and myself: for them at least the making of enough money to buy outright the big modern fishing craft which Marney had set his mind on, for the whole family to move, lock, stock and barrel to Whitby and its safe all-weather harbour.

Lobster and crab fishing, although seasonal, had always been one of the most lucrative pursuits of the inshore fishermen, not only along the Yorkshire coast but around the whole of the British Isles. The pots used varied in design. Those used by the south coast fishermen were chiefly bee-hive shape, woven with withies with a central vertical funnel or spout and very big, so that a score of them in a boat the size of the Lunn's coble would have been an awkward and dangerous load. They too were fragile, liable to destruction in stormy weather.

Nor was shell-fish fishing confined to the coasts of Great Britain. Lobsters, crabs, spider-crabs as well as the common sort, crawfish (the French langouste) were found along most of northern European coasts. Lobster fishing was a major industry in Nova Scotia and Newfoundland and other parts of North America. And all my enquiries went to show that with the exception of Japan, where the giant spider-crabs are caught in nets, the apparatus universally used was the bulky, awkward to stow and fragile pot.

While it was true that these pots were mostly made by the fishermen themselves, much of their material, twine and ropes had to be bought and, counting their labour, it was no exaggeration to put the cost of a single pot at fifteen shillings. This, Marney had informed me was the actual price paid by some of the Whitby fishermen who were engaged in intensive lobstering, using as many as four hundred pots. They had no time to make these themselves. They had to employ the old retired men of the port. Apart from losses of pots due to storms, the average 'life' of an ordinary pot was not more than three seasons. Over the years, in Great Britain alone, the total loss could amount to many thousands of pounds.

There could be little doubt then that a lobster-pot, with a frame made not of wood boards and hazel wands, but of iron, which would also fold flat when not in use, and yet could be erected easily and quickly would be of immense value to fishermen in any part of the world. Made of iron, it would need no ballast to overcome the buoyancy of the wood. For the same reason it would be lighter to haul. It would still require braiding, but even this could be woven on machines, and just need tying on to the frame. From the first, I conceived my apparatus as a subject for mass production.

It would not have required the genius of an Edison or a Marconi to invent it. Any village blacksmith or garage apprentice given the frame of an ordinary pot and told to design one in iron or steel with bows that would fold should have had no difficulty in doing so.

The base had to be made of angle iron similar to that used for a bed. By cutting out triangular notches or mitres at three points in the lower section of the 'L' the iron could be bent into a rectangle, riveted at the unmitred ends. The bows of iron rod would have their ends turned over so that they could be hinged into holes in the upright sections of the 'L'. If two of the bows were loosely coupled together by a thin, flat piece of iron at their top, they would fall together on to the base when not secured. And to secure them there would be another shorter piece of metal hinged to the top of the third bow, but fitted with a catch at its other end, that would snap on to the top of the middle bow. In place of the wooden slats on the ordinary pot there would either be thin strips of iron or wire netting.

I had made my first experimental model out of a discarded baby carriage, a parrot cage and an old iron bedstead I salved from the village rubbish dump across the green near to my cottage, labouring in a creative frenzy throughout the night with hack-saw, breast drill and hammer, and other tools that I found in my late ship's carpenter chest. But for the second practical model I had to seek the co-operation of the village blacksmith with his forge for the shaping of the bows with bent ends.

A bigger difficulty had been to adapt the main braiding and the spouts so that they would collapse when the bows did, and it had taken Marney many nights of patient experiment to solve a problem that would have beaten me. In the end it had seemed mechanically perfect. When the damaged pots had been repaired and fishing resumed we had given it a practical test. It could be opened and shut in three seconds. When, with the ordinary pots waterlogged, they had been shot on the close-in rocky grounds, we had proved that it would 'fish' just as well as them, for there were two lobsters in it the first time it was hauled.

My optimism then had been unbounded, and this I was sure was shared by my friends, although I did not disclose even to Marney my intention of buying them a super fishing craft as soon as the first money from my invention started rolling in. And they were not the only ones who were going to benefit by it. It could revolutionise the inshore fishing industry of Great Britain, and most likely that of many other countries where shell-fish were caught.

For the special benefit of British fishermen I visualised a huge co-operative business. A British Inshore Fisheries Corporation, manufacturing, selling or even leasing the pots to fishermen on easy terms: buying their catch at a fair price, distributing it, retailing it in the company's multiple shops and, if tremendously increased catches resulted in over-production, starting a shell-fish cannery. Everything would be profit sharing, and run on model lines. Indeed, I saw myself as a captain of industry, not with a Rolls-Royce—God forbid—but with an ocean-going motor yacht in which as a business man I could travel to various countries to demonstrate and sell the pot, further the interests of my company and, whenever I could find time, indulge my temporarily cooled passion for 'straight' fishing. Canada would take priority among the countries I would visit. I had never caught a salmon on rod and line. It would also be very pleasant to visit the West Indies, to renew my acquaintance with East and South Africa (I had spent some time in hospital in Cape Town after my crash). There were shell-fish, if not lobsters, certainly crawfish and crabs in the waters of all these countries, with an abundance of other fish.

Alas—it was not to be.

My invention failed, but not because of any intrinsic fault. I had a dozen of the frames made by a firm of engineers in Leeds. Although the mitre notches in the angle iron and the various holes which I had made laboriously with the breast drill were punched out with a machine, the bows and other parts had to be hand made. Because of this, and because I had all the frames galvanised to protect them from the corrosion of sea water, they were very expensive. But for mass production there would be special tools and jigs for bending the bows and hinge projections. The ultimate cost should not be more than five shillings, without the braiding.

The District Fishery Officer, representing the Ministry of Agriculture and Fisheries, was a man whose confidence and opinion I could trust. He had carried out a practical test of the pots in the Lunns' coble, and expressed strong approval in a report to the Ministry. But it was clear that I would need a lot of money and the co-operation of business people to get my company going, and having had no success with my writing for a long time I was then virtually broke.

I had a friend in London, however, who had a friend, a distinguished retired Indian Army general, company director and promoter who was also interested in the welfare of ex-servicemen. I had written to him in strict confidence—for I hadn't yet taken out even a provisional patent—telling him that I had invented an apparatus that should prove of immense value to the British inshore fishing industry (many of its men had rendered gallant service in the war) and in addition was likely to prove an extremely lucrative business proposition. I must have written very convincingly for after further correspondence, he had invited me to meet him in London at his city address, enclosing in his letter a cheque for my expenses. I took with me in a canvas case one of the galvanised pots, which Marney had braided with particular care and with untarred twine.

The General looked rather dubious when I took the pot out of its case, and laid it on his office table. The braiding was jumbled and without shape, the bows of course flat. But when with one quick and practised jerk I erected it and clicked the locking catch he was as surprised as if I had performed a clever conjuring trick. I had, of course, sent him a copy of the Ministry's report.

I could tell that he was deeply impressed. But he chilled me a little when he told me that none of the companies he was interested in would be likely to take it up nor could he do much himself at present as he was shortly leaving on an extensive business tour of the States. What I must do was to find someone who would put up the necessary capital to secure world patents and begin the manufacture of the pots, a sum of at least two thousand pounds. He would give me introductions to various persons in London who might be interested. In the meantime he was willing to advance me the sum of fifty pounds, on the understanding that this would be repaid when my circumstances permitted. This should keep me going in London for a time. . .

And here I can do no better than quote as the epitaph from a book that I was eventually to write, in which, with little elaboration of the truth, I told the story of the Walmsley Collapsible Indestructible

Lobster-Pot:

'I had started that search with unbounded optimism, not in any way discouraged by the fact that had his faith been like mine the General himself might have provided the requisite money. London abounded with millionaires and philanthropists and wealthy business concerns to whom the sum of two thousand pounds would be insignificant. One had only to stand at Hyde Park Corner and count the number of Rolls-Royces that passed in five minutes to realise it was no fairy tale that the streets of London were paved with gold.

'One had only to look at the palatial blocks of offices and flats and stores they were building, and the new tube stations, picture palaces and super restaurants, and in the six-wheel buses with their cushioned seats: one had only to watch the shopping crowds in Oxford Street and Regent Street and Kensington: or in the city, to see the silk-hatted bank messengers hurrying along with black bags full of money to realise that London was a city of stupendous wealth.

'It was as though one could hear through all the roar of the traffic, the stir and tinkle of a perpetual stream of money, welling out of the banks, spilling over the counters of shops and into the tills of restaurants and pubs and theatres and picture palaces: into the bags of bus conductors and the pockets of taximen, into the automatic tube ticket machines and cigarette machines, telephones and public lavatories; and flowing back to the banks where you'd see men in dark clothes with pale, bored faces shovelling heaps of coins with copper shovels, and moving thick wads of pound notes about with no more concern than if they were packets of cheap stationery. Yet the great electric cables buried under London's roadways are not more adequately insulated from irregular leakage than the main arteries and veins of this palpable river of cash.

'I lived in cheap lodgings in Brondesbury, overlooking the Queen's Park Station marshalling yard. Every morning I set off with my lobster-pot in its canvas case in my search for capital. Thanks to the letters of introduction given to me by the General I had interviews with millionaires, with titled philanthropists of renown. All these gentlemen seemed impressed by the pot when I demonstrated it, and by the fact that it had been praised by Government experts: all expressed deep sympathy with the British fishermen, but none offered to take a practical interest in the pot itself.

'On my own initiative I demonstrated it to the founder and managing director of one of London's biggest departmental stores: to a director of a famous shipping line, to a director of the Bank of England itself, without result. I secured admission to the inner office sanctuary of a famous financier who a few months later was to receive a long prison sentence for fraud. He had seemed more impressed than any of the other gentlemen for he owned a magnificent steam yacht and he said he would like to buy a score of my pots when I had them made, and try them on his next voyage to the Mediterranean. It was a sound proposition, but he was too busy with other matters to consider it at present.

'The great world slump was imminent, yet every day the advertising columns of the Press were full of the prospectuses of new companies. The public was invited to invest (and presumably was investing) in concerns for the exploitation of gramophones and records, of radio apparatus, of colour photography, cinemas, patent mattresses and medicines, greyhound racing tracks, dirt tracks and "take yourself" photography machines. It seemed to me that the whole country had gone pleasure mad: that people could think of nothing else but listening to the gramophone or radio, or going to the movies, or watching tame dogs chase an electric rabbit, or men falling off motor cycles or having themselves photographed in twelve different positions for a shilling in the slot.

'I did not despair however. I would look at every fishmonger's slab I passed on my daily pilgrimage, and often I would stop and enquire the price of lobsters and crabs, and the smell of fish was enough to keep me in mind of my purpose. The sight of enormous cooked lobsters, draped with parsley and garnished with slices of lemon in the window of a famous Piccadilly restaurant inspired me with the thought that one day I might see such lobsters stamped with the trade mark of my company.

'Spring passed and summer came. I had long since exhausted my advance and there was no sign of the General's return. I got a part-time job with an advertising company however which kept me going, and for a fortnight I earned a princely salary looking after a stall at a trade show in Olympia, only for this I had to hire a black jacket and striped trousers from Moss Brothers. I did not relax my search but I changed my tactics. It occurred to me that my invention and its associated schemes had a wider aspect than the purely commercial one.

'A Labour Government was in power. I wrote to the Minister of Agriculture himself, explaining how I had failed to obtain the necessary capital to put the manufacture of my pot on a practical basis, and suggesting that it might be a subject for State subsidisation on co-operative socialistic lines. I did not get an encouraging response. I wrote to the ex-Minister of the Conservative Opposition, thinking he might find some excellent party counter-propaganda in the scheme. I got no reply at all.

'I remembered that there was a Member of the House of Commons whose whole career had been devoted to the interests of deep-sea fishermen and was known as the Fishermen's Friend. I wrote to him, and he asked me to have lunch with him at the House, and bring the pot along. He gave me an excellent lunch. My pot was opened and shut within sight of several other distinguished Members of Parliament and although I saw them giving it interested glances our conversation was not disturbed.

'My host, he was the Tory Member for Grimsby, was very sympathetic. But he saw no hope for me in subsidisation, a word of terrifying significance to any Member of Parliament, whatever party. What I wanted, in his opinion, was a wealthy man who liked publicity and would not mind paying to have a few thousand pots made and *giving* them to the fishermen, as long as the world knew who had done it.

'I did not imagine that the General was the sort of man to do that. Throughout that summer and into autumn however he was my one remaining hope. In the meantime there had been a sensational criminal case which as the newspapers said "rocked the whole structure of British finance to its foundations". It concerned the very gentleman who owned the steam yacht.

'I did not know whether the General had been

involved in that financial disaster which had ruined so many investors and speculators, or if it was this that had brought him back to England. He was busy, and I had to wait several days before he could give me an appointment. He was kind to me, almost fatherly, but he told me frankly that in the present state of affairs, with a world-wide depression setting in, my chances of securing financial backing for my pot were nil, that he himself could help me no further.

'It was dusk when I left his office near Leadenhall Street. I had my pot with me in its canvas case. I wandered east through the city, paying little attention to where I was going until I found myself in Mark Lane, and I smelt the river. I walked on past the Tower Moat, and on to the Tower Bridge, and halted at last in one of those bays where the pedestrian may stand and look down into the Pool of London. The wind was easterly, and there was a smell in it that was not that of the river only and of ships, and merchandise and smoke but of the sea itself. It was raining and cold, with the wind blowing in gusts, and I was the only person standing in the bay so that—waiting for a gap in the stream of vehicular traffic—I could have slipped over the balustrade, without a soul being the wiser.

'But I had no mind for suicide. The feel of that wind in my face, the smell of the distant sea had aroused in me a furious desire to be back in Bramblewick among my fishermen friends, even if I had to tell them of my failure; to smell the real sea again, to hear the sound of the breakers on the scaurs, to hunt for rag worms to fish with my old sea rod.

'I suddenly saw that I had done with my patent lobster-pot for ever. I lifted it over the balustrade of the Tower Bridge and I let it drop into the cold, dark and lobsterless Pool of London.'

23

I WROTE that book, which I called *Phantom Lobster,* and the one that preceded it, *Three Fevers,* at Fowey, in circumstances which I have recorded in a third book, employing in each a certain amount of 'poetic licence' but with *Phantom Lobster* sticking more closely to the truth.

I had left my beloved Bramblewick because I had got rather heavily into debt (I had received no less than five writs in one week from the County Court bailiff) and I had chosen Fowey as it was as distant from my creditors as I could get in England. I was eager to settle with them all, but I couldn't do it if they were to bother me like this. I had been told too that the fishing at Fowey was very good.

Although the first book had been surprisingly well received by the critics, neither it nor the next one had made much money. It was the sale of the film rights of *Three Fevers* to the newly formed British National Films, the chairman of which was millionaire Arthur Rank, with multi-millionairess Lady Yule as co-director, that brought me back to Yorkshire.

Here it would give me great pleasure to record that at last I was able not only to pay off all my debts, but to buy for my friends the super fishing boat that Marney had dreamed about. They indeed had been more on my conscience than the creditors. Although they had taken the failure of the pot philosophically I had a feeling that I had led them up the garden path with it. Huge sums of money were paid to authors for the film rights of their books. This, however, was in Hollywood. It was with the highly moral purpose of ousting the glamorous sexy Hollywood film that Arthur Rank, who was a Sunday School teacher as well as a race-horse owner, had started this company. He intended to produce clean British films. Mine was a nice clean British book, which although there were one or two swears in it might safely be given as a Sunday School pnze.

The sum I was offered, and accepted, for the film rights was three hundred pounds, with a 5 per cent royalty on net profits. I would in addition be paid six pounds a week as technical adviser during the production. I wasn't going to buy a super fishing craft out of this! But it was assumed that although the characters in the film would be played by professional actors, the fishermen would co-operate in the production, doubling for the dangerous rough sea sequences. They would of course be paid for this and the use of their boats and gear, more I imagined than they would be likely to earn from their winter long lining, unless things had improved since the days I had fished with them.

I was in for a big surprise. My friends the Lunns had left Bramblewick and moved to Whitby. They had acquired a brand new Scottish-built fishing boat similar to those about which Marney had spoken so enviously, fully decked, with a wheel-house, a cabin with a galley stove and bunks for a crew of four, equipped with a powerful diesel engine, giving it a speed of eight knots and supplying current for cabin lights and deck floodlights for night fishing.

Whether they had bought it outright, or, overcoming Mrs. Lunn's scruples, put so much down, the balance on instalments, I never discovered. Certainly it was with no financial help from me and the profits from my patent lobster-pot. It was theirs, and they were making plenty of 'brass' as Marney had said they would, 'potting' for lobsters and crabs, long lining in deep water, trawling, drifting for herring, all according to the seasons. Certainly they were better business men than I had proved to be!

Yet, if they were proud of their boat, which at Mrs. Lunn's own suggestion had been christened *Easter Morn,* success had not gone to their heads. They were as friendly as ever. They were still using some of my 'shut-up' pots with the four hundred of their own they were working, but because there was plenty of room on the deck of *Easter Morn* they never bothered to shut them up. They had tied the locking bar 'permanent'. Shut-up pots really were only used for small craft like their old coble. For them it was a champion idea!

It would take a whole book to describe in physical and psychological detail the making of that film which in due course was to be shown to the public with the title *Turn of the Tide* with a brief acknowledgement that it was based on the novel *Three Fevers* with my own name added. It may be true that an author should have nothing to do with the filming of his own book. If he sells the film rights he should have the transaction carried out entirely through an agent, and never under any circumstances meet any person con nected with the film company, and make up his mind from the start that the script writer, the producers, the director will do precisely the opposite to what he would do himself if he wished to convey his story, its plot, characters and atmosphere through the medium of talking moving pictures. Also that if he has feelings about his story—and between some authors and their books the relationship approaches that of mother and child—he will resist the temptation to see the film when it is made, unless he has nerves of iron.

My case was different. I knew that film making was an entirely different medium from writing. I did not imagine that *Three Fevers* could form anything but the basis for a film. I wasn't highbrow either in my conception of it. First and foremost the film should be entertainment, something the public would pay money to see and enjoy. Yet as it was to be about fishermen, I wanted it to portray them and their activities authentically, avoiding the silly things one so often saw in Hollywood films. For that reason alone I would have gladly taken on the job of technical adviser even without that six pounds a week.

My book was a plain record of a year's fishing activities in the village, the 'fevers' being the enthusiasms for the next season's fishing as one declined, lining in winter, lobsters and crabs in early spring, salmon in the summer months. All I had done in the way of invention was to increase the rivalry between the two families of fishermen to a feud—the old-timers against the 'foreigners', a feud temporarily forgotten when it came to manning the lifeboat to carry out a salvage operation for a ship that had gone ashore in a fog, an operation in which I actually took part myself, sharing in an award of one hundred pounds.

The book had no plot. The sea itself was the protagonist. There was no love interest, beyond the happy family life of Marney. Although written first person throughout the narrative, I was the unnamed ghost. My patent pot did not come into it, of course.

Into this simple story, for box-office appeal there was injected an elderly member of the Fosdyck family to be known as Old Isaac, possessed of a fierce hatred of the Lunns, and capable of breaking all the rules of fisherfolk behaviour by cutting the buoys from the Lunns' lobster-pots. He had a beautiful granddaughter Ruth, so that she could be a Juliet to John Lunn's Romeo.

Lovely Geraldine Fitzgerald, straight from Dublin's Abbey Theatre, and possessed of a charming Irish brogue, was to play the part of Ruth. John Garrick as John Lunn was to be her Romeo. Niall MacGinnis, Marney; Sam Livesey, father of equally famous Roger, Henry; Hilda Davies, Mrs. Lunn; Joan Maude (daughter of Nancy Price), Marney's wife; and the late Derek Blomfield, then a boy actor, had the part of Stevie, the Lunns' mischievous youngest son.

For the Fosdyck family the fine old Shakespearian actor, Fisher White, was to play Old Isaac. Wilfrid Lawson (later a magnificent Doolittle in the film *Pygmalion)* was to play Luke Fosdyck, with Moore Marriott as his brother Tindal. The real Lunns, after some persuasion agreed to co-operate. They would be paid for their services, the use of their craft and loss of fishing time.

The real Luke and Tindal had retired, and had sold their coble, leaving Oliver to earn what he could with a small summer pleasure boat, and two old Whitby fishermen were engaged with their sailing coble to stand in for Luke and Tindal, although Oliver was put on the payroll for crowd scenes. Luckily the Lunns' small coble, which had been sold to a Whitby fisherman, was available. It was brought back to its old harbourage in the Dock, to be launched down when action demanded.

Production started in early March and for the next six weeks the old village, which at this time of the year and especially with no fishing going on would normally have been deserted, was a bedlam of commotion. Apart from the cast and the fishermen, the camera and sound crews and other members of the company, there were crowds of spectators eager to watch the film stars at work. There were autograph hunters, newspaper reporters and photographers. It should have pleased me to be asked for my own autograph even when the hunter having signed up Wilfrid Lawson went on to beg the same favour from the company's carpenter. It should have pleased me to be interviewed by the reporters, to see a photograph of myself, arm in arm with lovely Geraldine in the *Daily Mail.* It did and it didn't, for soon I began to suspect that the whole thing was going to be a flop.

It became clear that my job as technical adviser was to be nominal. There was a sequence taken from the opening chapters of the book where the cobles are cod fishing in winter. A storm comes on. The Fosdycks rush ashore, but the Lunns hold on to the last moment and have to make a hair-raising passage into the Landing. We had the good fortune to have such a storm. With seas actually breaking across the Landing mouth, the real Lunns in their old motor coble imperturbably made the passage out, the coble at times almost on end, turned and came back again, Sam Livesey, Garrick and MacGinnis, changing oilskins with them as soon as they reached calm water. And they repeated this performance for three 'takes'.

But this scene had to be linked with one showing the anxiety of Marney's wife and Ruth as they stood watching the boat from the cliff edge. It couldn't be done the same day. It was not until the storm was over several days later, that both girls, in spite of my protests, were posed on the cliff overlooking the Bay. By then the wind was blowing strongly offshore, with scarcely a ripple on the sheltered Landing. True, they made a striking picture as they stood with the wind blowing their hair, while they registered first terror and then relief as the coble was supposed to make the perilous passage already filmed. But Hollywood I felt, could not have perpetrated anything sillier.

I wasn't happy. Neither were the Lunns. They had not objected to my 'using' them in my books, copies of which, of course, I had sent them. I didn't know how much the company was paying them. The arrangement had been made through the secretary-paymaster, but they had made no complaint about the terms to me, and I assumed it was satisfactory. But the sight of Sam Livesey and Garrick and MacGinnis, masquerading as themselves, doing and saying things that no fishermen would ever do, must have been irritating. What was getting them down more than anything, however, was the waiting, the interminable periods of inactivity, when there was 'nowt' to do, while most of the time the *Easter Morn* was lying idle at her Whitby moorings.

Such waiting I knew was inevitable. I was well aware that Norman Walker, the director, had taken on a very difficult job. There was no electricity supply in the village. It had been impossible to obtain a portable generator to produce current for Kleig lights. Filming could only be done in daylight and with the sun shining. Some of the sequences needed a rough sea, others, like the shooting and hauling of pots and lines, needed tolerably smooth conditions, and this was the North Sea and it was still winter. It would take perhaps a whole morning to prepare for one shot. There would be a rehearsal, with the actors saying their lines with the appropriate action, over and over again until the camera man and 'sound' were satisfied. Then the long wait for the sun to come out from behind the clouds, and if it didn't the shot would have to be postponed to another day.

The Lunns, of course, were not aware to what extent the film version was to diverge from the book. They hadn't read the script. If they had, they might well have refused their co-operation in the finale, in which with themselves 'unseen' the *Easter Morn* was shown leaving Whitby Harbour for the fishing grounds with Luke Fosdyck (Wilfrid Lawson) at the helm, and in command Tindal (Moore Marriott), Henry (Sam Livesey), Marney (Niall MacGinnis) and John (John Garrick) in various attitudes on the deck, but all of them grinning and waving their hands to Old Isaac, Ruth (Geraldine) and Amy (Joan Maude) grouped amicably together on the pier ends, waving them *bon voyage.*

By then, of course, the feud between the two families had been resolved. Not only had vindictive, Lunn-hating old Isaac seen the evil of his ways, but he had put up the 'brass' for the Lunns and Fosdycks to go into partnership in a new boat, and given his blessing to the marriage of Ruth and John, an ending most definitely not that of the book, or real life.

In spite of our differences I liked and admired Norman Walker, and I was sorry for him, for I could tell that his heart was in making the film a big success. But when, with all or at least most of the outside location sequences in the can the company packed off to Elstree to complete the making of it in the less rigorous but probably more phoney atmosphere of the studio, I was left with the sure conviction that nothing they did there could possibly save it from being an absolute failure. God knew what the critics would make of it if it ever did reach the screen as I sincerely hoped it never would, and that if it did, the Lunns at least would never see it. They'd never forgive me.

*

But it did ultimately reach the screen at a Saturday morning trade show, followed by a celebration luncheon party at the Savoy (attended by Arthur Rank and Lady Yule) to neither of which I was invited. Perhaps because of this slight, I waited with a somewhat malicious anticipation, for the slashing of the film would get in the Sunday papers.

The first notice I read was by Miss C. A. Lejeune in the *Observer*. Her column was headed ENGLAND AT LAST. She summed up a long detailed review with: *'A sane, salty story, beautifully presented, beautifully photographed, with a kind of spring fever over trees, sky and water, lovely and exciting, impossible to overpraise.'*

Sydney Carroll, then film critic of the *Sunday Times,* was even more enthusiastic: *'It is impossible to avoid superlatives. A perfect example of technical skill, artistic direction, and ideal casting.'*

But there was not a single Sunday paper film critic who did not rave about it, and the daily newspapers next week were no less enthusiastic: *The Times, Daily Telegraph, Daily Mail, Express, Chronicle,* and *Daily News*.

Alistair Cooke, then film critic for the B.B.C., said on the air (his talk was later reproduced in the *Listener*):

'Turn of the Tide *is likely to give you more pleasure than any film that has been made on this blessed isle. . . It has some beautiful acting, especially by Geraldine Fitzgerald. After Hollywood has tricked out its sirens with the last secret of sex appeal, along comes a plain girl in a woollen sweater, takes one frank look at a fisherman she loves, and leaves you swooning in your seat from literal excitement. . . Norman Walker, who directed this film has only another eight weeks to go before his anxiety can be relieved at having turned out the best British film of the year.'*

Had all these so-called critics gone, mad, I wondered? Was it the champagne at the luncheon party that had turned their heads? They were all Londoners of course, completely ignorant of fishermen and their ways. It would take hard-headed Yorkshire folk, the fishermen themselves, people who lived in close contact with the sea to recognise, for example, the utter absurdity of that shot of the two girls with their hair streaming out in the west wind, pretending they were watching the coble riding in on the breaking rollers of a north-easterly gale. And there had been several 'takes' made against my 'technical' advice equally incongruous.

In due course *Turn of the Tide* came to Whitby. For a whole fortnight it topped the bill at the Empire cinema, and was watched by wildly enthusiastic audiences, among them all members of the Lunn family. They loved it, every minute of it, even that last phoney scene of the *Eastern Morn* steaming out of the harbour with everyone smiling and waving their hands and this to the accompaniment of soft fade-out music.

I saw it myself. I was, and perhaps remain, the odd man out. The photography was superb. Some of the shots of the sea and the coast and the old village were as beautiful as anything I had ever seen on the screen. The shot of the coble coming in to the Landing was breathtaking. I agreed with Alistair Cooke, that Geraldine Fitzgerald shone with her beauty and her acting, although she did not make me swoon in my seat. I agreed, too, with Sydney Carroll about the technical skill and artistic direction. It is true, too, that in the cliff-top scene with the two girls, they made such an entrancing picture, that I forgot to look at the sea itself. And I did not notice until someone pointed it out to me later, that when a lobster-pot was hauled up, the lobsters in it had their claws tied, and that what was meant to be a live salmon was actually a rubber one supplied by the studio effects' department.

It did not bother me a bit that the film bore little resemblance to the book. But where it did fail was that it did not in any degree get over the men themselves, either the Lunns or the Fosdycks. I was watching actors and actresses all the time with only the sea authentic. And yet it undoubtedly was first-class entertainment, and by all the rules should have made another fortune for its millionaire producer and a moderate fortune for me out of my 5 per cent royalty on net profits.

It did neither. The hold of Hollywood on the British cinema industry was too powerful at that time. *Turn of the Tide* was never shown as anything but a 'second feature'. Its profits never got near to its product costs. And yet it made history for undoubtedly it was its commercial failure that inspired Arthur Rank to fight and ultimately defeat the barons of the film world. It was the foundation of the Rank Empire!

24

IT was not until the excitement of the film had died away that I made my first fishing trip in the *Easter Morn.* How different it was to prove compared with that freezing winter's day at Bramblewick when I had first gone out with the Lunns in their coble to watch them shoot and haul their lines.

It was early summer, when crabs and lobsters cast their shells and are virtually out of season. The herring shoals had not yet arrived along the north-east coast. The pots had been brought ashore. This trip was to be 'netting and overing', something I had heard about but never witnessed, for it was deep-water fishing impracticable for the coblemen.

The 'netting' meant shooting herring nets, not to catch herring but mackerel, on the principle of a sprat to catch a mackerel, a mackerel to catch a whale, the 'whales' in this case being the cod and other fish my friends were hoping to find on a ground a long way out from the coast, a ground which Henry had 'struck' during the war when he'd been skipper of the mule. It was rough ground, too rough for the steam trawlers. As it was well out of sight of land it could only be located by the compass, by the speed of the boat and by the passing of time measured by the wheel-house clock. There were occasions during the war, Henry had told me, when he had caught as many as forty stone of prime haddock on that ground as well as other fish, but of course other times when there was next to 'nowt', but then it always was like that with fishing!

It was dusk when we cast off from the fish wharf, and moved down the harbour between Whitby's ancient piers, and I couldn't resist saying to Henry, who was in the wheel-house, the door of which was open:

'What did you really think when you saw *Easter Morn* steaming out to sea with Wilfrid Lawson at the wheel pretending to be old Luke?'

He laughed.

'Why—it was nowt but a lot of daftness from beginning to end and there were dafter bits than that—I could have split my sides when I saw that chap MacGinnis pretending to be our John, hauling up a pot and taking out a lobster that had its claws already tied. But it was a good film for all that. That bit with us coming through the Landing came out well, didn't it? I wouldn't mind seeing it all over again. But I'm not sorry them days with us fishing from Bramblewick are over and done with. This is a different carry on, isn't it? No launching up and down, and being able to stay out all night, and plenty of room for all our pots when we come to shift them, although I still think that shut-up pot of yours was a good idea.'

Marney had joined us.

'Listen to him cracking up this against Bramblewick. Do you remember how he used to tell me to hold my jaw, if I ever dared to mention going in for a bigger boat and flitting to Whitby?'

Henry laughed.

'You'd best hold your jaw now. We couldn't have left poor awd Luke and Tindal and Oliver to go by theirsens. We had to wait till they retired, and there was plenty of other reasons too, and we needn't go into 'em again.'

I still hadn't discovered how they had come to possess the *Easter Morn*. It was clear that it was a private matter, yet I could have no doubt that to all intents and purposes it was theirs, and I had confirmation when John put his head out of the engine-room hatch and shouted:

'Eh—come and have a look at this.'

We had reached the pier ends with their lighthouses. The boat began to rise and fall to a long lazy swell. I stepped down into the engine-room, room a misnomer, for the massive engine seemed to occupy all the space. It was illuminated with a dazzling electric light.

'What do you think of it?' John said. 'An improvement on our old Kelvin, eh? But it's still a Kelvin—their latest diesel model. Eighty horse-power. Starts at a touch, and it'll tick over to keep us moving at less than a couple of knots. Eight knots full out. There's a throttle control from the wheel-house, too. You can shut up the hatch, and never bother to look at the engine again till we're back in port.'

I knew very little about engines, but I was impressed by all that John had told me. It was undoubtedly a good engine, and it was a good boat, but no better than my friends deserved. The twin piers were already well astern when I returned to the deck.

It was a lovely evening, warm with no wind. The sky was overcast but it was with an even stratum of high static summer cloud without menace. The swell was just enough to give an easy fore and aft sway to the boat. We were moving straight out to sea, the lights of Whitby swiftly receding, but with the lights of ships appearing ahead as we drew near to the coastal traffic lane.

Darkness fell and by then there were no visible lights astern. Marney and John had moved into the bows, and were lying prone, staring down into the water. The bow waves were blue with phosphorescence but clear of the waves there were also gleams of phosphorescent light, and suddenly Marney gave a shout to Henry at the open wheel-house window:

'Here they are. Either mackerel or herring. Slow down!'

The boat slowed so that the bow waves became scarcely more than a ripple from the stem. The flashes away from it were now more apparent, but I could not have told that they were made by fish. It was clear, however, that Marney had no doubt.

Both he and John stood up. A powerful deck floodlight was switched on. Then Marney picked up the big bladder buoy of the net piled amidships, threw it over and with John started to shoot, the boat now moving at half speed. I was still the amateur, still the impotent spectator, but I knew that in this type of fishing, no anchors were used. The net simply formed a curtain fifty feet deep, supported by corks at short intervals, and with larger bladder buoys at longer intervals. The fish were not enclosed, as with a seine net, but were meshed as they swam into the net from either side. When shot, boat and net would be allowed to drift with the tide, the boat using her engine only if the wind was unfavourable, and then only in occasional gentle bursts of speed.

Now we had no wind, and there was no need to hoist the sail which, tight hauled, would have kept the boat head on to it. A drifter fishing for herring would use anything up to eighty nets, each a hundred and fifty feet in length, and making one continuous 'curtain' extending three miles. We were only using two bent together, and the shooting was done in less than twenty minutes. Half an hour later the hauling began.

There was no doubt that Marney had been right about the fish. They came in by the score, meshed on both sides of the net, still alive and kicking, all good-sized mackerel. They were shaken out on to the deck and I was able to help by picking them up and throwing them into a big fishbox. This and another were full to overflowing when the end of the net came in. The engine was opened up again and we were steering seawards once more, while Marney and John began the job of cutting the fish up, bait size.

By now we had company in the shape of a number of herring gulls, superbly beautiful in the light of the lamp, flying so near to the boat and the fish that they had to be shooed off from making a grab. We were still moving at full speed. It must have been close on midnight when at last we slowed down. We had evidently reached the fishing ground. The marking buoy, a much bigger one than we had used with the inshore lines, went overboard, followed by a heavy anchor. The shooting began in silence but for the steady throb of the engine and the squawking of the gulls. Marney was at the line, John by his side with a boat-hook in his hand to stop the impudent gulls seizing the baited hooks as Marney cast them over, Henry ever watchful, looking out of the wheel-house window ready for action if anything went wrong.

There were eight lines, each with five hundred hooks. As one was shot, its end was bent on to the free end of the next, by John, and it was while he was doing this that one of the gulls dived down and snatched a beak full of (fortunately unhooked) baits, the rest of them screaming after it to rob it and, but only temporarily, leaving the shooting to be carried on undisturbed. It was not until the last line was shot, and the bait box empty that they finally gave it up.

As Marney threw the marking buoy over he shouted, half to the buoy and half to me:

'That's that. And now for a sup of tea and summat to eat afore we start hauling. There's half an hour yet till daybreak. I've a mind for a fried mackerel. There's still a few left we haven't cut up. Let's get down to the cabin. I banked up the fire afore we left port. Kettle ought to be boiling.'

The cabin hatch was forrard of the hold. The galley stove was on. It was stifling hot and there was a powerful smell of bilge, enough with the movement of the boat to have discouraged anyone with a squeamish stomach from partaking of a meal, especially mackerel fried in bacon fat, and accompanied by almost black tea. But I was hungry and not too squeamish, and if Marney's cooking was not up to the standards of his wife, I enjoyed the meal, in which John too shared without any complaint. The boat was still under way at half speed with Henry in the wheel-house steering, I assumed, back to the first buoy. I was puzzled that when we had done eating neither of his sons showed signs of going to relieve him. I knew it would be silly for me to offer.

'Isn't Father coming down?' I asked.

Marney laughed.

'Not him. You wouldn't get Father coming below while we were at sea, and especially eating owt even if he was hungered to death, and it's a cosy spot this, especially in winter time. Don't let on to him, but I reckon it makes him feel sea-sick. Queer, with him having been at sea all his life.'

'Why, there's lots of fishermen and sailors too like that,' said John. 'To tell you the truth, I've sometimes felt queer myself when we've been rolling a bit, stirring up the bilge. Of course not in calm weather like this. Isn't it time we started hauling? I wonder if we're going to get owt like a catch.'

'Not if you start your bloody croaking,' Marney snapped.

The time had come. When we got out on deck the eastern sky, although still overcast, was grey with the approaching dawn. There was no wind. But for the long swell we might have been on a mountain-sheltered lake. There was enough light for us to see the first buoy not more than a length ahead of us. Marney picked it up with the boat-hook, hauled in the slack of the warp into the sheaves of the line hauler, geared with a clutch to the engine. John put the clutch in. The hauling began, with the boat moving slow ahead.

Evidently it was very deep here. It was a long time before I saw through the clear bottle-green water the white gleam of a fish, and then the anchor. The anchor came in first. The fish, several bare hooks along the line, was a haddock, about a couple of pounds. Marney didn't use the gaff, and John, who was paying the line as it came from the hauler into one of the baskets, unhooked it without comment. Several more bare hooks came in. And then there was an extraordinary sight. As deep down as I could see below, the line looked like a washing line hung with garments blowing and flapping in a wind. But as it was hauled the 'garments', distorted by the refraction of the water, became the shape of fish. And they were not haddock. The first one which Marney gaffed and swung over the gunwale on to the deck was a cod, as big and if not bigger than the one I had caught at the Billet Scaur. It was followed by another and at least half a dozen more, without a single bare hook.

I moved to help with the unhooking, but I was waved aside by John.

'We don't trouble about that. Hooks are cheap enough.'

He simply gave the snoods a jerk, threw the fish aside, and did the same with the next to come aboard. And still the line as it rose through the pellucid water gleamed with more and more fish.

Without looking round Marney shouted to his father:

'It looks as though you've put us on the spot all right.'

'I thought we couldn't be far off, if the clock was keeping right time. But we won't know for certain till the fish stop coming in. That'll show we shot off the rough ground.'

But as the hauling continued there came no sign that this had happened, or was likely to happen. There were bare hooks, but very few, and always there was at least one fish in sight coming to the surface. They were not all cod. There were ling, one that must have weighed at least thirty pounds. There were several big skate, and one big conger, which John greeted with a muttered curse. When we came to the second line there was a 'run' of more than a score of haddock, all on consecutive hooks, all the same size as the first one caught. These at Marney's request I collected and put into a fishbox. The big fish were simply left to slither about on the deck. It would have taken time to stow them in the fish hold.

There were more cod, although not quite such big ones on the fourth line, and then a 'run' of dog fish, which if once despised by the fishermen and only used for pot bait, now had a market price. And as if these had scared the other fish away, there came a succession of bare hooks. But it didn't last long.

Marney gave a shout, and this time I knew he wasn't joking:

'There's a big 'un coming up. Stand by with your gaff, John.'

I saw the familiar gleam of white again. It came nearer, a fish weaving from side to side, white one moment, brown the next.

'It's a skate,' I said.

'Skate be damned!' Marney shouted. 'It's summat better than that. Stand back. Stop the winder, John.'

I stood back. John had declutched the winder. He and Marney bent over the gunwale, and then heaved over it on to deck, a huge fish, which although I had never seen caught before I recognised as a halibut. Even John was moved to an outburst of near ecstasy, as he whipped the snood from it.

'By gum—that's a bit of luck. Sixty pounds if it's an ounce. There's at least three quid's worth there. You've put us on the spot all right, Father!'

Henry, who had put the engine into neutral and was leaning out of the window, smiling:

'Aye,' he shouted. 'But I've had bigger ones than that on this ground. Get on with your hauling. There might be another yet.'

It wasn't angling. I would have been thrilled to have hooked and landed a fish like that, or the big ling for example, on rod and line. And I was still only an onlooker. What did that matter? It was just as exciting, and all the time I was thinking of what this was meaning to my friends in terms of cash. I had watched the selling of fish from time to time on the Whitby Market. There were occasional gluts of course, but an average price for cod was twelve shillings a stone, haddock fourteen shillings, and in times of scarcity, crabs might fetch twelve shillings a stone, lobsters as much as twelve shillings *a pound.* Those big cod, and there were at least fifty of them already, must be worth at least ten shillings apiece. And now there was the halibut.

Turn of the Tide! I had thought that title to be as phoney as the film itself. But the tide had turned for my friends after the years of hard going at Bramblewick: the poor catches, the good catches cancelled out by losses of gear, and the periods of enforced fishing inactivity due to stormy seas, and the barrier of the Landing.

It wouldn't always be like it was today. The winter months would come, lining and potting. But the harder the weather and the scarcer the fish, the better the market price for what they caught, and with a boat like *Easter Morn* and a harbour like Whitby's there would be few days of 'doing nowt'. They were business men. And it looked to me that the only thing left to bother them now would be the enemy of all business men, the Income Tax inspector!

25

WHILE there were no record-breaking heat-waves, the Cornish summer of 1964 was warm and dry with plenty of sunshine for the holiday-makers. There were no gales or thunderstorms. The inshore sea was consistently smooth. Yet from June until the end of September, there was not a single day without a wind blowing from some direction, mostly from the north or north-west, never more than fresh, but except on very few occasions strong enough to make an excursion to the whiting grounds, either in the dinghy with George Sully's outboard or in *Amanda,* a hazardous proposition.

Actually we did try it again with the dinghy, the throttle of the engine now repaired so that we could go at any speed from full-out to slow. We started catching mackerel as soon as we left the harbour mouth, but before we had got halfway to the ground and out of the lee of the land, the north wind was raising a 'chop' which, farther out, I knew would make things too uncomfortable for fishing, and we turned back. Once, with the water in the harbour and along the cliffs dead calm, I set off alone in *Amanda.* I had no sooner reached the ground and dropped anchor than I felt the first puff of offshore wind. The fish were there all right, the same big whiting, hooked two at a time as soon as the sinker touched the bottom. But before I had caught a dozen the wind had freshened. *Amanda* was rearing up and down to the short steep waves, dragging the anchor.

If, and this was always possible, I had engine trouble I might be blown out to sea, and suffer the indignity and the possible expense of being 'rescued' by a passing coaster or professional fishing boat, towed in perhaps to Mevagissey or Par or Polperro or Looe. I hauled the anchor and made for home.

On the next occasion, and this time George was with me, the wind was blowing very gently from the west raising scarcely more than a ripple on the water. The sun was shining, visibility excellent, so that there was no doubt that with Punch Cross in line with the red roof and Daphne's watchhouse just clear of Pencarrow Head, we were on the exact spot where we had made that huge catch of whiting. On the way out we had caught several mackerel. With these for bait, it looked as though we were going to repeat that performance. We 'fished' for four hours. In that time we tried fishing farther out and farther in, farther east and farther west. We tried just drifting. We did not get a single bite.

The winds of that summer were, of course, just what the amateur yachtsmen who flocked to Fowey in the holidays wanted, and particularly was this so in Fowey's regatta week. And they made no difference to Bill Haley, who day after day, and always precisely at six o'clock would come into the Town or the Albert Quay, to disembark his 'clients' and then carry up to Percy Varcoe's shop his huge pollack and boxes of silvery bass.

How did he do it? Was it that echo sounder of his, or some special sense that told him precisely where the big fish and the bass were to be found? I would see him fishing in various places, sometimes far out, sometimes close in, east or west along the coast, sometimes anchored, sometimes just moving slowly round and round, evidence that he had found either pollack or bass. But if I tried that place after he had moved on it would never be with success. True that he invariably fished with the best bait for both pollack and bass, live sand eels caught with a purse net on the up-river sandbanks opposite to Golant.

These too could be caught without a net, but it was a devil of a job. It had to be done on the ebb tide, as soon as the sandbanks were exposed. The sand was coarse, loosely packed, so that you couldn't dig it with a fork, as you did in mud for rag worms. You had to use a spade, using it at the edge of the receding tide and work fast, for the slightest movement would send the sand eels burrowing deeper into the sand. If you lifted one out with the spade it would jump madly about either to get back into the sand or into the water. You had to chase it, hold it, drop it into your bait box and shut the lid.

Yet sand eels were well worth the trouble. Early one morning I pulled up the river in the dinghy bent on getting some. And there was Bill, just hauling in his net, helped by two young visitor lads. His big boat was anchored in deep water. His rowing boat, from which he had shot the net was ashore near to where he was hauling. The lads were some yards up-river hauling at the net's other warp, and clearly they were finding it too heavy.

I grounded my dinghy near to Bill and got out. Here was a chance of getting some eels without the fag and uncertainty of digging for them.

'Can I help?' I said to Bill innocently.

'Thanks,' he said. 'My mate hasn't turned up. If you can pull on the other end where those lads are doing their best.'

The corks of the net made a semicircle still some distance from the shore. I joined the lads, and with

Bill hauling on his end, the net slowly came in. As it did so we moved nearer to Bill until with the first corks ashore we were alongside him. We were soon hauling on the net itself, making two piles, the semicircle diminishing. The meshes so far were too big for sand eels. We hadn't reached the small meshed 'purse' but already at the apex of the diminishing circle I could see an agitation in the water, sand eels, and prawns, too, jumping clear of the corks, as the mullet had done with my own net. But not many escaped. Hauling quicker the last corks came in. The purse was dragged ashore clear of the water. And there inside it was a mass of jerking, jumping eels, prawns too, and several small mullet. Bill opened the lid of a big box.

'Do you lads want the prawns?' he said. 'You pick 'em out if you do, but look quick.'

Evidently the boys had been prawning when they had come to Bill's assistance. Their nets and buckets were on the beach. I helped them sort out the prawns. Bill threw them the mullet too. I was waiting hopefully for my own small share of the booty, and I felt diffident about asking. Perhaps it hadn't occurred to Bill that I had come up with the intention of digging for eels. With the prawns clear I helped him lift the purse so that the eels poured into the box in a silvery cascade. He shut the lid. I helped him carry it into his boat. I helped him too, to stow the net into the boat, and it was not until this was done that he said:

'What are you doing today? Are you busy writing books or were you going fishing?'

It looked like being a fine day. I *had* work to do, but it was more likely that we'd be having one of our picnic bathing teas on one of the beaches with trolling on the way. Bill had given me a lead in however. All I wanted was a score or so of eels.

'I *am* a bit busy,' I said. 'But I was hoping to get a bit of fishing some time. I came up in the hope of digging a few eels as a matter of fact. I've got a box in the dinghy.'

'Why, you can have as many eels as you like. No need to dig for them.'

And then he astonished me.

'I just thought that if you weren't fixed up, you might like to come out with me and a nice old gent who's booked for a day's fishing. It would be a change from fishing in your small boat. We'll be leaving the Albert at ten sharp, back at six, so you'd want some grub. What do you say about it?'

I had an instant vision of those big pollack, of bass galore, of fishing grounds I'd never dared to venture to in *Amanda.* I had a slight twinge of conscience, when I thought of my wife and daughter, but they could have the dinghy and I was far from being indispensable on a bathing picnic expedition. My answer was yes.

26

ALTHOUGH I had known Bill Haley for many years, I had always felt a little shy of him. He lacked the easy affability of the local Cornishmen, the boatmen, shipwrights and boat builders, the ferrymen, the workers on the china-clay jetties. Although 'local' for generations, he had no trace of the Cornish brogue in his speech. He had joined the Royal Navy as a boy, seen service in many parts of the world and had risen to the rank of chief petty officer before retirement. But always his hobby had been angling, and he had found a profitable outlet for this on his present occupation. I knew this mostly from hearsay; from his more communicative and charming 'missus', Bea, and his pretty married daughter Melita, who had a daughter the same age as Selina, and a son who was the small 'spit and image' of Bill himself.

Bill was a fine-looking man, now in his early sixties. There was still something of the Royal Navy about him with his cheese-cutter cap, his neat black jersey, his polished black shoes. Everything inside the boat, too, was neat and shipshape, spotlessly clean, ropes coiled yacht fashion, so unlike *Amanda*. And I was still a bit shy of him, finding it hard to believe as we moved out of the harbour mouth at full speed that I was actually bound on a day's fishing with him and this 'gent' whom I will call Mr. Brown.

Unlike some of the gents I had seen embarking

on Bill's boat armed with expensive-looking fishing rods, landing nets, gaffs, creels, tackle boxes, there was nothing sporting in his appearance. He was elderly, short, rather tubby with a pleasant clean-shaven face, and kind blue eyes. His hair was white, but he was wearing a woolly cap on his head, collar and tie, a loose-fitting alpaca jacket, nondescript trousers. Lacking only an apron I could have taken him for a village shopkeeper. All that he had brought with him, in a string shopping bag, was a large thermos flask, and a parcel of food. It was part of Bill's 'service' to supply the fishing gear as well as bait for such clients who did not bring their own.

Yet Mr. Brown was no amateur angler. I was to learn that he was one of Bill's 'regulars' that this was an eagerly looked forward to annual event for him. Fishing had been his life-long hobby. But he lived in an inland town where he owned a small business: where the only available angling was for coarse fish in canals and gravel pits, to be shared with other anglers. It was better than nothing, but not to be compared with the sea angling, the big pollack, the bass of Fowey. Besides, there was the sea air, the beautiful views, the pleasure of being on a boat like Bill's, the certainty that there would always be something to catch. Bill never let you down!

I was uncertain whether Bill intended to let me join in the actual fishing, or whether he had merely invited me as a spectator, to impress me with his boat and his professional skill. Tactfully I had not brought my own fishing gear. Certainly I was impressed with the boat, especially the roominess after the cramped space of *Amanda*. She had been specially built for safe, comfortable sea angling. She was twenty-four feet in length, one third decked, providing a day cabin with a lavatory, and space for gear. Abaft the cabin the deck was raised to form a glazed 'dodger' or canopy, giving ample headroom and protection for the steersman and passengers, compass and instrument board, including the echo-sounder apparatus. The engines, there were two of them, 6-8 h.p. petrol burning, were bedded well down below the open deck, their casing lid forming a convenient table. With a nine-foot beam there was plenty of room to walk about.

I didn't care much whether I fished or not. I was happy. It was a perfect summer's day with the sky blue with cotton-wool clouds throwing purple shadows on the cobalt of the sea, and only momentarily masking the sun. True, there was a wind, cool and from the north, the same old wind that would have made things uncomfortable for *Amanda* at the whiting grounds. I wouldn't have that to worry about today; whether I was going to find any fish or not, or have engine trouble, or get lost in a fog. It was pleasant to think that for once someone else, and more competent than I, was holding the baby, and that it wasn't my baby anyway!

We turned west from the harbour mouth on a course slanting seawards from the coastline over ground familiar to me from innumerable excursions both in the dinghy and *Amanda.* We passed Coombe, where a hundred yards out from the cove, trolling at dusk in *Amanda,* I had caught my own record pollack of ten and a half pounds, on a handline of course. That for Bill would only be an average-size fish. By how much I wondered were we going to beat that today?

He had switched on the echo sounder, chiefly I thought to impress me, for he must have known every inch of the sea-bed so close into the coast. But it was fascinating to see its inked pointer tracing on the broad, moving ribbon of calibrated paper, the contour of the invisible ground below us. For the breadth of Coombe it ran almost level. Then, where I knew there was a reef reaching seawards, on which I had often fouled my trolling line, it rose sharply, then quickly fell again, and continued almost level until we opened Pridmouth Bay; when it rose again. And it was then that Bill cut out one of the engines and reduced the speed of the other to dead slow.

I was puzzled. We were still only within easy pulling distance of the harbour. I had fished here many times myself without notable success. There were several already mounted rods neatly arranged on a rack near the dodger. They were like my own rod, fibre-glass, only longer, and furnished with conventional reels. Bill selected one and handed it to Mr. Brown, who was seated in the stern.

'I think this is the one you had last summer when we struck the bass at Lantic Bay. I doubt if we'll find any here but we can give it a try.'

Mr. Brown smiled. I sensed his excitement.

'The very one, Bill,' he said. 'My lucky rod, eh?'

The sand eels were in a big cask of sea-water. With a little net Bill scooped one out, threaded the hook of the line through the thin integument of the eel's lower jaw, then pulled the hook through and impaled it in the skin of the belly close to the head. The line was thin gut (10 lb. breaking strain Bill told me) with a single light movable sinker. Mr. Brown took it, and with the boat still moving dead slow, he threw the bait over, paid out the line. Bill selected another rod, baited it and to my embarrassment handed it to me.

I didn't know what he charged his clients for a day's fishing. Certainly it would be considerably more than Captain Bunny's 'bob an hour' that would have to be defrayed by Mr. Brown. In boat fishing it is not inevitable that the angler with the most skill, with the best gear and bait, catches the most or the biggest fish. I recalled an occasion when fishing in the *Lydia* with Captain Bunny and a 'party', I had caught fish after fish while the others weren't getting a bite. One of the men in the party had made me change lines with him but I still went on catching them while he got none. It would indeed be embarrassing if the same thing happened now, and deliberately I paid out my bait very slowly, sincerely hoping that no fish would see it. But before it was out of sight Mr. Brown was winding in. Bill moved to his side with the landing net. He didn't use it however. The fish came in sight and Mr. Brown simply swung it on board. It was a mackerel. While Bill was unhooking it I struck one too, and brought it in.

Bill didn't look pleased.

'I was afraid of this,' he said. 'There's not often been so many mackerel about as there has been this summer. They're a nuisance. We don't want to waste eels on them. We'll move on.'

The close-in sea was dotted with small pleasure craft, motor, sail and pulling, many of whose occupants would be indulging in the sport of mackerel fishing, with spinner or the now popular 'feathers', a deadly device used by the commercial fishermen, and anything but sporting. It consisted simply of a heavily weighted handline, with as many as a score of hooks spaced at short intervals on a trace of stout synthetic gut, terminating in the sinker. The hooks were tied, trout-fly fashion, with brightly coloured feathers, which, trolled or jerked up and down, fooled the fish into thinking they were living sprats or sand eels. When a boat struck a shoal the lines might be hauled with a mackerel on every hook.

Bill didn't re-bait. We moved on, round the Gribben out of sight of Pridmouth and the Fowey coastline into St. Austell Bay. The north wind was stronger now, and there were short, white-tipped waves which would have caused *Amanda* to cavort uncomfortably. But we were as steady as if we'd been in the harbour. There was a magnificent view, with the coastline sweeping round from the sandy beaches of Par and Carlyon Bay to Black Head, Mevagissey and the distant Dodman, past which the ships of the Spanish Armada had once passed in full sail. Inland on the skyline beyond St. Austell the china-clay pyramids gleamed white in the sun. Mr. Brown, who, Bill had warned me, was not talkative, was moved to say:

'It's pretty this, one of the prettiest sights I know. I often think of it when I'm at home.'

'It'll look prettier when we sight something different from mackerel,' Bill said grimly. 'We'll have another try.'

He baited Mr. Brown's line again, and it went over. He gave me an eel and I baited my own while Bill himself took a rod, baited it and let it go over. Almost simultaneously we struck fish. They were all mackerel. Bill made no comment. He did not re-bait but opened out the engine, started the second one, and we turned at full speed straight out to sea.

We had gone about a mile when the echo sounder indicated rising ground, but at a depth of more than twenty fathoms. Bill cut one engine, and dead slow on the other, moved round in a circle, his eyes all the time on the sounder needle. We came astern a bit, then we stopped, and he threw a heavy anchor overboard. In silence, he baited Mr. Brown's line, handed me an eel, then he began to bait his own. We had swung round with the wind to the cable. With the check off his reel Mr. Brown was allowing his bait to go straight down, and Bill said to me, laconically:

'Let it go to the bottom, then raise it about a fathom, We're after pollack now, not bass.'

I did what I was told, but again deliberately, I kept my finger on the reel checking its descent so as not to get ahead of Mr. Brown. I saw him wind in a little, proof that he had reached the bottom. And then as I did the same, I saw him give his rod a jerk. It bent. He started to reel in.

Bill was watching him too.

'Have you got him?'

Mr. Brown had stood up, winding slowly, the rod bending and straightening alternately.

'Yes,' he said. 'A nice fish, too.'

Bill was still holding his own rod, with the landing net in easy reach and he was watching Mr. Brown. I felt a savage jerk on my own rod. I struck, and to my relief, realised that I had missed the fish. The bait would be gone. There would be no fear now of my out-shining the fish that was coming in. The water was very deep. It was a long time before Mr. Brown shouted:

'Here it comes, Bill!'

I hadn't bothered to wind in my own line. I could see the fish, not more than two fathoms down, by its dark-green back and golden belly unmistakably a pollack. Bill leant his rod against the gunwale, grasped the landing net. But as he did so his own rod jerked violently. He shouted to me:

'Hold on to it, will you?'

I leapt across and gripped it, felt the tugging of a big fish, and I just held on while Bill took a stride astern, dipped the net into the water and swung Mr. Brown's fish safely on board. Then he came back to his own rod, and started winding.

I moved astern to look at the fish. Mr. Brown was beaming. It was a pollack, bigger, but not by much, than my own record ten pounder, not so big as some that I had seen Bill land on the quay, but a beauty. It had swallowed the hook, and it would be for Bill to disgorge it. We were both watching him now. His fish was fighting hard. From time to time he was just holding on, taking its weight with the rod, then winding faster. Was it going to prove bigger than the other one? I dared to hope that it wouldn't. I saw it at last, but it was not until Bill netted it and swung it on board that I knew it was going to be a close thing, for it seemed identical with the one that Mr. Brown had caught. They looked like twins.

Bill unhooked them. He weighed them with a spring balance. The first was exactly twelve pounds. His own, unless he was fiddling the balance, was two ounces under, a win for Mr. Brown. Our lines were re-baited, and over the side again. My wished-for ill luck held. For before I had touched bottom I felt a fish, struck it, hauled it in. It was a mackerel.

There were no more really big pollack however. There were plenty of fair-sized ones, up to six pounds. I caught one that Bill thought worthy of weighing and it touched eight, a fish that would have surprised and delighted me had I been fishing in the dinghy or *Amanda.* An hour went by. Then came the mackerel again, seizing our baits before they reached the bottom. Bill hauled the anchor, started both engines, and we turned at full speed east back towards Fowey, but still well out to sea.

In twenty minutes we had almost reached the

whiting ground. I reminded Bill of how he had 'rescued' me in the fog that day and I told him too, without going in to details how George Sully and I had subsequently found it, and caught the big whiting. He listened in silence, but as the hut came in sight beyond Pencarrow Head, he picked up a pair of field-glasses, stared at it, then looked shorewards to Fowey, where Punch Cross was just visible with my naked eye, showing against the red roof.

'This is about it, isn't it? It's a long time since I've bothered with whiting.' Then he turned to Mr. Brown. 'Would you like to have a go at the whiting for a change? We could anchor here and have our grub before going on to the Udder.'

'That's all right, Bill. I'm feeling a bit peckish.'

The engines were stopped. The anchor went over. The wind was now fresh, the waves so steep that I would have been really scared in *Amanda.* But as we swung round to the cable the boat rode level. The wind was scarcely noticeable in the lee of the canopy. This was luxury fishing, with the only disadvantage that there were no fish, not even mackerel. It meant at least that we could eat our sandwiches and drink our coffee without distraction. In half an hour we were under way again, now steering for Lantivet Bay, east of Pencarrow, where a mile out from the shore there is a sunken reef marked by a Trinity House bell buoy, known as the Udder.

One of the long local fishing boats, owned by a friendly young man, Mike Digby, was cruising round close to the buoy. He had a party of four visitors on board. Bill hailed him:

'How are you doing, Mike? Any bass?'

Mike was grinning.

'Not a stinker! Plenty of damned mackerel, and a few pollack, but nothing big. How have you done?'

Bill held up Mr. Brown's pollack. There were envious looks from the members of the party.

'One more a bit smaller than this,' Bill said. 'About a mile off the Gribben. But no bass.'

We moved on well clear of the other boat and shorewards. With fresh eels on all three lines we started fishing again. And then the very thing I didn't want to happen did so. I hooked a fish, and I knew that this time it was no mackerel. It was pulling too hard for that. I was aware that both Bill and Mr. Brown were watching me intently. I hoped for Mr. Brown's sake that it was only a pollack, smaller than his own. My hope was quickly dashed. It was not a pollack but a bass, only a quarter the size of that big pollack, but to any angler more desirable. Bill lifted it into the boat. I felt like apologising. Why, oh why, had it taken my bait instead of Mr. Brown's?

But Mr. Brown himself was now winding in. Another bass? One bigger than mine? Again my hope was dashed. It was only a small pollack, and as Bill unhooked it (I was unhooking the bass myself) I imagined that he must have been making an envious comparison. I could only hope that I wouldn't catch another.

I didn't. We fished for an hour round about the Udder, getting only pollack, some so small that they were thrown back. I began to wonder if for once Bill's sixth sense was going to fail him. Or was I going to prove a Jonah? His echo sounder was of no value here. With our lines aboard we set off again at full speed, east and well out to sea. We had steamed for more than half an hour when he slowed down and switched on the sounder. We were about two miles from the coast. He cut one of the engines, reduced the speed of the other until we were barely moving. His eyes were on the sounder needle however. It was indicating level ground, then suddenly it shot up into a point, and quickly down again. He put the helm hard over. We came back on our track, and the pointer moved up again. He reversed the engine, we lost forward way. With the recorder marking the highest point he cut the engine, heaved the anchor over. We started fishing again.

Was it the echo sounder, or Bill's sixth sense? Mr. Brown had no sooner got his line to the bottom than he was winding in another big pollack. It was not quite so big as his first and before Bill had time to unhook and weigh it, his own rod was jerking. But I had one myself too, luckily only a six pounder. Bill's wasn't a pollack but a ling, sizeable but still not challenging Mr. Brown's twelve-pound pollack. And as in the first place where we had fished we went on hauling fish in as fast as the deep water, the unhooking, re-baiting, permitted, all apart from Bill's ling, pollack, none less than four pounds, three, all of which Mr. Brown caught, round the ten-pound mark. And still his record remained. And yet apart from my own, there was not a single bass. At last the fish stopped biting. Bill glanced at his watch. It was after four o'clock, and we were at least an hour's run from home. I knew that he never varied his duration of fishing time, ten o'clock out, six o'clock back to the quay.

'It's time we packed up,' he said. 'But we'll have another shot at the Udder on our way back, and try Lantic Bay.'

But we were only halfway back to the Udder when Bill picked up his glasses, and looked seawards with them where a long way out, and just visible to the naked eye, was a flock of sea-birds, wheeling over the water.

'There's a shoal of fish out there,' he said. 'It's most likely mackerel again, after sprats, but you never can tell. We'll go and have a look.'

He steered towards them, and there flashed through my mind the time that Captain Bunny had sighted the gulls on that wonderful day in the *Lydia*, when we'd struck the first mackerel shoal. It was as though I could hear his voice telling me to throw the spinner over and start fishing. As then, as we drew nearer, I could see that there were gannets and black backers and guillemots and other sea-birds among the gulls, some wheeling round, some diving, some swimming on the surface, but there was too much 'chop' to see whether there were any breaking fish.

Were they just mackerel? They were the last fish we wished to see today, but on that occasion with Captain Bunny the mackerel had been only the prelude. There had been the gurnard, the billet, the cod and even the flatfish when we'd anchored. A hundred yards short of where the birds were concentrated, Bill slowed to minimum speed. He baited Mr. Brown's line, and I saw it go over before I followed with mine. Bill remained at the helm steering to one side of what apparently was the shoal. We were trolling, of course, with only short lines, so that the baits would not be more than a fathom from the surface.

I felt a tug. I struck. And at the same time Mr. Brown shouted:

'Got one.'

'Is it a mackerel?' Bill shouted.

He was reeling in, his rod whipping. For the first time there was real excitement in his voice.

'No—I think—yes, *it's a bass*!'

I hung on to my own fish, not really caring whether it was a bass, pollack or mackerel, or whether I caught it or not. I had the joy of seeing Mr. Brown's fish come on board, a four-pound bass, glittering like a bar of silver. I hauled my own in then with a clear conscience, glad all the same that it was a smaller one than his.

Bill had lived up to his reputation. We, or rather he, had found the bass, Mr. Brown hooked another as soon as his line was over again, and it was the same with mine. It was clear that what had attracted them and the sea-birds, was a shoal of pilchard fry, the Cornish equivalent of our Yorkshire herring sile, and actually sardines. As we unhooked the bass, the fry spilt from their mouths, little pilchards three inches long. It was exciting. Fish after fish came in, all bass, none bigger than four pounds, but none small. I was no longer worried about Mr. Brown. I did suggest to Bill however that he might let me take the wheel so that he could fish. He laughed and shook his head.

'You carry on,' he said. 'I like to see other people hauling 'em in. Anyway, the sand eels are nearly finished,' and then he added, still laughing: 'Have you ever had fishing like this at that spot of yours in Yorkshire?'

I thought of Captain Bunny and the *Lydia,* that lovely summer day. 'Only once, Bill,' I said, 'and it was a mighty long time ago.'

Perhaps if he reads this book he will know what I meant.

About the author

LEO WALMSLEY was born in Shipley, West Yorkshire, in 1892, and was brought up in Robin Hood's Bay on the North Yorkshire coast — the 'Bramblewick' of several of his novels. After serving with distinction in the Royal Flying Corps in the Great War, where he was awarded the Military Cross, he determined to become a writer, beginning with boys' adventure stories.

He lived for a while in London before returning to Robin Hood's Bay in the late 1920s, then settled in Fowey, Cornwall and wrote *Three Fevers* (1932), the first of his 'Bramblewick' novels, followed by *Phantom Lobster, Foreigners, and Sally Lunn.*

In addition to over twenty books, he wrote 200 or so short stories and articles prior to his death in 1966.

For further information about
Leo Walmsley, or membership
of the Walmsley Society,
please visit:

www.walmsleysoc.org